MAKING SAUSAGE
OUR AMERICAN VALUES AT WORK

Maryanne Kearny Datesman

Dedicated to my husband George, my daughter
Lisa, and my granddaughter Olive

TABLE OF CONTENTS

PREFACE

The last few years have been really tough, causing many of us to ponder who we are and what our life priorities should be. On a personal level, we may face economic uncertainty and family challenges. On a national level, we are subjected to increasingly acerbic debate about who we are as Americans, and what our national priorities should be.

Since co-authoring *American Ways: An Introduction to American Values* with Edward Kearny and JoAnn Crandall, I have given a lot of thought to American values. First published in 1984 as an English as a Second Language reading textbook, and now in its 4th edition, *American Ways* is designed to help non-natives understand what makes Americans tick.

It has been used by American embassies around the world to help their native employees understand Americans' beliefs, motivations, and cultural values, and at various times it has been used by the Peace Corps, State Department, and several other government agencies.

My dear husband George has been after me for over 30 years to write a non-textbook version specifically for Americans, and this is it: *Making Sausage: Our American Values at Work.*

Why now?

A majority of Americans are now concerned about the state and future of the very democracy that *is* the United States of America. Historians, political experts, pundits, and just plain citizens decry the lack of ordinary civility, and everyone seems to agree that finding common ground should be a national priority.

The purpose of this book is to remind us of what makes us "Americans"—our unique cultural values—where they came from, how they developed, and what has been their impact on our lives.

There is something truly extraordinary about the cultural values of the United States—a power that has allowed us to accept immigrants from all over the world and enable them to become "Americans."

What is the source of this power? Is it still working today, or have we lost our sense of common identity?

What are our ideals? Are we living up to them? Do they still matter?

These are important questions, so let's consider them together. Join me in watching the sausage being made, as we explore the messy process of living up to our highest ideals and what makes us "Americans."

"Some of you are here to make a beautiful pâté but we're making sausage most of the time."

— Speaker Nancy Pelosi, quoted by CNN, addressing the House Democrats, July 10, 2019

"The sausage is made."

— President Biden, "Remarks by President Biden on Passage of the Bipartisan Infrastructure Bill," November 6, 2021

INTRODUCTION

When I was a child, my grandfather took me to a hog butchering on the family farm. I'll spare you the images burned into my memory, but suffice it to say, it was several years before I could eat sausage again.

The phrase "watching sausage being made" implies some messy, unpleasant process of accomplishing an important task. The quote is attributed to Otto von Bismarck. "Laws are like sausages; it is better not to see them being made."

The early 2020s could well be remembered as "the years of making sausage."

Four crises emerged in the summer of 2020: a coronavirus pandemic, a resurgence of the quest for racial equality, an unsteady economy, and a bitterly divided electorate.

Added to this, there were serious questions about the Federal Government's response to these crises. Some argued that it did not adequately address these critical problems, while others bemoaned government intrusion into their private lives.

The challenges the United States faces may vary from year to year, but one thing is clear. Finding acceptable solutions to national problems is a messy process in our democracy.

The *good news* is that our Founding Fathers set up a system of government that has allowed our country to deal with crises, dissent, and even a bloody Civil War.

- *As the Constitutional Convention of 1787 drew to a close, Benjamin Franklin was asked what he thought the Convention had produced. "A Republic," he replied. And then he added the cautionary words, "If you can keep it."*

- *Happily, Americans have kept it, so that today the United States has become the only nation in history to maintain a constitutional system of ordered liberty for more than two centuries. But the system and its liberties are not a perpetual-motion machine that can run indefinitely without the attentions of the American people.*

> *In each succeeding generation it is necessary to develop a firm understanding of the core documents of American liberty—the Declaration of Independence and the U.S. Constitution, including the Bill of Rights—and a reasoned commitment to their values and principles.*
>
> From the Preface to the *2018 Civics Framework for the National Assessment for Educational Progress (NAEP Civics)*

The *bad news* is that many Americans are either ignorant of or have forgotten these basic values and principles.

How do Americans learn the basic values and principles of our democracy?

One would assume that this information is taught in American schools. The standards for what students should know at various grade levels are, in fact, articulated in the Civics Framework for the 2018 National Assessment for Educational Progress (NAEP Civics) cited above.

The NAEP Civics document also describes the assessment that should be administered to students at grades 4, 8, and 12. It is

> *designed to measure the civics knowledge and skills that are critical to the responsibilities of citizenship in the constitutional democracy of the United States.*

The assessment is a not a national test, where individual students' or their schools' scores are reported, but rather a "survey-based barometer or broad indicator of how much and how well students are learning."

Due to limited funds, only the eighth-grade students participated in the last assessments in 2014 and 2018, and **only 24 percent demonstrated civics proficiency.** That is to say, students could understand and explain:

- *Differences between government and civil society, and American ideals and reality*
- *Separation of powers among branches of government*
- *How citizens can influence government*
- *Events that have international consequences*

According to the NAEP Civics report, civics education is sorely lacking in many American schools today, in spite of requirements stated by school districts and state departments of education.

- Less than half the states require secondary school students to take even a one-semester course in civics or government.
- Students in K-8 get some information about civics and government

in their social studies classes, but these topics lack substantial treatment.

- As for American history courses, these tend to emphasize social history, with little attention to political history, the founding period, or the development of the Constitution.

Why is it so important to understand civics and the story of the founding of the United States?

Because this shared narrative tells us *who we are* and reminds us what our country stands for.

- Our ancestors came to America for freedom and a better life for themselves and their children.

- They created a totally new nation with an innovative system of government designed to protect their liberty and the free lifestyle they desired.

- As a result, a system of *cultural values* evolved that became the guiding principles of our nation.

This book will define and explain each of these cultural values in detail.

It is critical to remember that these are *aspirational* values, *ideals* that are imperfectly realized.

How well have we lived up to our cultural ideals?

Perceptions vary. Certainly there are obvious inequities in the United States today, with 40% of the wealth in the hands of the top 1%.

- Those leaning liberal may see the glass as half empty, emphasizing the plight of the poor and the minorities in the United States, and how they have been denied the promised ideals of our founding documents.

- Those leaning conservative may see the glass as half full, emphasizing that we need to embrace our traditions and take pride in the progress we have made in achieving success and building a great nation.

What is the purpose of this book?

In this time of chaos and confusion, we need to stop and remember who we are and what our country stands for.

The purpose of this book is to remind us of what makes us "Americans"— our *unique cultural values*—where they came from, how they developed, and what has been their impact on our lives.

There is something truly extraordinary about the *cultural values* of the United States—a power that has allowed us to accept immigrants from all over the world and enable them to become "Americans" and new citizens.

Think about that. Throughout our history, immigrants have introduced countless different languages and varied cultural traditions, and yet our fundamental "American-ness" has endured for over 200 years. We have a recognizable national identity.

Where did this cultural identity come from?

It all started with our founding documents.

The Constitution begins:

WE THE PEOPLE of the United States, in order to form a more perfect union, establish justice, insure domestic tranquility, provide for the common defense, promote the general welfare, and secure the blessings of liberty to ourselves and our posterity, do ordain and establish this Constitution for the United States of America.

But in 1787, "WE THE PEOPLE" did not include enslaved African-Americans, indigenous peoples, or women.

We have been working ever since to achieve "a more perfect union," striving to include *all* Americans in "WE THE PEOPLE," and endeavoring to make our ideals more of a reality.

Living up to these ideals is a continuous, never-ending struggle, and securing the blessings of liberty and justice for all is often a messy process, like watching sausage being made. Thankfully, however, our unique cultural values are still at work.

Question: For you as an individual, what is the most important thing about being American?

SOURCES

Civics Framework for the 2018 National Assessment for Educational Progress, published by the National Assessment Governing Board, U.S. Department of Education

https://www.nagb.gov/naep-subject-areas/civics.html

https://nces.ed.gov/nationsreportcard/about/organization_governance.aspx

https://www.nationsreportcard.gov/civics

https://nces.ed.gov/nationsreportcard/civics/

https://www.americanprogress.org/article/state-civics-education/

https://constitutioncenter.org/media/files/constitution.pdf

Chapter 1

ARE WE REALLY THAT DUMB? THE PAST IS PROLOGUE.

Collegestats.org published a list of 25 American History facts most students don't know. On the steps of the Lincoln Memorial in D.C., students were asked why President Lincoln was important to America.

One student answered that his beard made him important; another said he was killed at a puppet show. Few were able to explain his leadership and role in the American Civil War.

YouTube is full of random "on-the-street" interviews about basic American history and civics facts, from Jay Leno's Jaywalking to Watters' World, with Jesse Watters, a Fox News host. The questions are simple, but the various answers are amazing!

- ***Who was the president during the Civil War?***
  The guy with the really tall hat. Lyndon B. Johnson?
  George Washington?

- ***Who won the Civil War?***
  Is that a trick question?
  New England?
  I'm not a fan of history, cause I don't believe it.

- ***What was the war called where we declared independence?***
  Civil War.
  Not the Civil War.
  World War II?
  The Renaissance?

- ***What country did we declare independence from?***
  Virginia?
  France? The South?
  Iraqis, I don't know—Iran?
  I'm not a history buff. Europe? France?
  The motherland, pretty much. America.

- ***Do you remember what year we declared independence?***
  No.
  1946. No—it can't be.
  1973? Was it?
  1737?
  1984?
  I really don't pay a lot of attention to history; it bores me to death.

- ***Who was George Washington?***
  He was the second president. After Lincoln.
  He was a general or something. He didn't work with horses, did he?

- ***Can you name one of the original colonies?***
  Boston.
  Alabama?
  Puerto Rico.
  Oregon?
  Arkansas?
  Philadelphia?
  Kentucky?
  America?

- ***The 13 stripes on the flag. What do they represent?***
  Freedom. Everything—like being free and being happy. Getting what you want.

- ***How many stars are there on the flag?***
  32? It's blowing in the wind so much I can't count them.

- ***How many Senators are there in the US Senate?***
  I think it's like 7 or 12. I'm not sure.
  I know this—50?
  10.
  52.
  Like 300 something?
  There's about 25. Or more.
  Oh, I'm not even going there. I'm so bad at this stuff.

- ***Who was the president during World War II?***
  Theodore Roosevelt? JFK?
  Ronald Reagan?
  Like Nixon or something? I don't know.
  Oh, my God. George Washington?

- *Who did we fight in the Cold War?*
  Turkey?
  The president means the turkey? The cold cuts? And then we call it cold cuts, cause we won the Cold War.

What conclusions can we draw here?

- It appears many Americans lack a rudimentary knowledge of basic American history and facts about the United States.

- You may have heard that the average American cannot pass the basic civics test required to become a citizen.

- We can laugh out loud at the answers to these questions, but many of the questions are taken from this citizenship test.

The Woodrow Wilson National Fellowship Foundation recently conducted a national study of how Americans score on citizenship test questions:

> *Unfortunately this study found the average American to be woefully uninformed regarding America's history and incapable of passing the U.S. Citizenship Test. It would be an error to view these findings as merely an embarrassment. Knowledge of the history of our country is fundamental to maintaining a democratic society, which is imperiled today.*

Americans need to understand the past in order to make sense of the present, and anticipate the uncertainties of the future, they concluded.

> *History is both an anchor in a time when change assails us and a laboratory for studying the changes that are occurring. It offers the promise of providing a common bond among Americans in an era in which our divisions are profound and our differences threaten to overshadow our commonalities.*

Question: Does it really matter how much we know about our history? Why?

SOURCES

https://collegestats.org/2012/07/25-american-history-facts-most-students-dont-know/

Jay Leno
https://www.youtube.com/watch?v=WJlY9C7YWzI

Jesse Watters
  https://video.foxnews.com/v/4341050883001#sp=show-clips

https://www.youtube.com/watch?v=OOGlv3T9SRU

https://hechingerreport.org/most-mississippians-cant-pass-u-s-citizenship-exam-is-american-history-education-the-problem/

https://www.pewresearch.org/politics/quiz/what-do-you-know-about-the-u-s-government/

Chapter 2

ENTRY LEVEL CIVICS: WHAT DO YOU KNOW?

Imagine that you are an immigrant to the United States. You have come here legally and are now ready to become a citizen. But first, you have to demonstrate a basic knowledge of U.S. history and government. You have to pass the Civics Test.

The test is administered by a USCIS (U.S. Citizenship and Immigration Service) officer, who will ask you 10 questions in English. You must answer 6 of the 10 items correctly (also in English) in order to pass this exam.

The queries are taken from a list of 100 possible questions that have the answers provided, so you can study for the test. You are expected to give one of the choices on the list, even though you may know additional information. For example, "What is *one* thing Benjamin Franklin is famous for?"

The possible answers are:

- U.S. diplomat

- oldest member of the Constitutional convention

- first Postmaster General of the United States

- writer of "Poor Richard's Almanac"

- started the first free libraries

Flying a kite with a key in a thunderstorm is *not* one of your options.

Nervous about taking the exam? You can take practice quizzes that have multiple choice answers online, but remember—*the actual Civics Test is NOT multiple choice.*

So, are you ready for your naturalization interview?

Welcome to the Civics Test!

1. What does the Constitution do?

2. The idea of self-government is in the first three words of the Constitution. What are these words?

3. What do we call the first ten amendments to the Constitution?

4. How many amendments does the Constitution have?

5. What is the "rule of law"?

6. The House of Representatives has how many voting members?

7. Who is your U.S. Representative?

8. The Federalist Papers supported the passage of the U.S. Constitution. Name <u>one</u> of the writers.

9. Under our Constitution, some powers belong to the states. What is <u>one</u> power of the states?

10. What is <u>one</u> responsibility that is only for United States citizens?

Well, did you pass? (See the answers below.*)

If you did, you are among *only one in three* Americans who are able to get a passing grade—answering 6 out of 10 questions correctly. According to a survey done by the Woodrow Wilson National Fellowship Foundation

- *Only 13 percent of those surveyed knew when the U.S. Constitution was ratified, even on a multiple-choice exam similar to the citizenship exam, with most incorrectly thinking it occurred in 1776.*

- *More than half of respondents (60 percent) didn't know which countries the United States fought in World War II.*

- *And despite the recent media spotlight on the U.S. Supreme Court, 57 percent of those surveyed did not know how many Justices actually serve on the nation's highest court.*

The survey also found that:

- *Seventy-two percent of respondents either incorrectly identified or were unsure of which states were part of the 13 original states;*

- *Only 24 percent could correctly identify one thing Benjamin Franklin was famous for, with 37 percent believing he invented the lightbulb;*

- *Only 24 percent knew the correct answer as to why the colonists fought the British;*

- *Twelve percent incorrectly thought WWII General Dwight Eisenhower led troops in the Civil War; 6 percent thought he was a Vietnam War general; and*

- *While most knew the cause of the Cold War, 2 percent said climate change.*

It is important to note that *the survey test was multiple choice—respondents had answers to choose from. However, the actual government citizenship test that immigrants take *is not*. They are only given the questions.

So, what information is on the Citizenship Test? What does the U.S. government say that immigrants should know in order to be granted citizenship?

Here is an outline of the 100 Civics Questions and Answers, prepared by the U.S. Citizenship and Immigration Services:

AMERICAN GOVERNMENT

    A. Principles of American Democracy

    B. System of Government

    C. Rights and Responsibilities

AMERICAN HISTORY

    A. Colonial Period and Independence

    B. 1800s

    C. Recent American History and Other Important Historical Information

INTEGRATED CIVICS

    A. Geography

    B. Symbols

    C. Holidays

You can look at the complete list in the Appendix, or online.

Did the Woodrow Wilson National Fellowship Foundation survey find any differences in the scores of older and younger Americans?

- *Surprisingly, the poll found stark gaps in knowledge depending on age.*

- *Those 65 years and older scored the best, with 74 percent answering at least six in 10 questions correctly.*

- *For those under the age of 45, only 19 percent passed the exam, with 81 percent scoring a 59 percent or lower.*

Question: Which age group do you belong to? What is your experience? Why is there a history/civics knowledge gap between those over 65 and those under 45?

SOURCES

https://woodrow.org/news/national-survey-finds-just-1-in-3-americans-would-pass-citizenship-test/

https://www.nbcnews.com/news/latino/most-us-would-fail-u-s-citizenship-test-survey-finds-n918961

https://my.uscis.gov/en/prep/test/civics/view

https://nces.ed.gov/nationsreportcard/nqt

Citizenship Interview
https://www.youtube.com/watch?v=SDb9_CqPUTQ

https://www.uscis.gov/citizenship/find-study-materials-and-resources/study-for-the-test/100-civics-questions-and-answers-with-mp3-audio-english-version

***Here are the approved responses to the questions above. Remember, *these are the only correct answers*:**

1. What does the Constitution do?
   - Sets up the government
   - Defines the government
   - Protects basic rights of Americans

2. The idea of self-government is in the first three words of the Constitution. What are these words?
   - We the People

3. What do we call the first ten amendments to the Constitution?
   - The Bill of Rights

4. How many amendments does the Constitution have?
   - Twenty-seven (27)

5. What is the "rule of law"?

   - Everyone must follow the law.
   - Leaders must obey the law.
   - Government must obey the law.
   - No one is above the law.

6. The House of Representatives has how many voting members?

   - Four hundred thirty-five (435)

7. Who is your U.S. Representative?

   - Answers will vary.

8. The Federalist Papers supported the passage of the U.S. Constitution. Name <u>one</u> of the writers.

   - (James) Madison
   - (Alexander) Hamilton
   - (John) Jay
   - Publius

9. Under our Constitution, some powers belong to the states. What is <u>one</u> power of the states?

   - Provide schooling and education
   - Provide protection (police)
   - Provide safety (fire department)
   - Give a driver's license
   - Approve zoning and land use

10. What is <u>one</u> responsibility that is only for United States citizens?

   - Serve on a jury
   - Vote in a federal election

https://www.uscis.gov/citizenship/find-study-materials-and-re-sources/study-for-the-test/100-civics-questions-and-answers-with-mp3-audio-english-version   (Last visited November 11, 2022)

Chapter 3

WHO ARE WE? DO WE HAVE A COMMON IDENTITY THAT TRANSCENDS POLARIZATION?

There is no doubt that we are living in a time of extreme polarization. Many decry the bitter partisanship and the hyperbolic rhetoric of our political campaigns, for example, but it is not new. Negative campaigning was in full swing by the end of the 1700s.

> *If Jefferson were to be elected, one Connecticut newspaper announced, "murder, robbery, rape, adultery and incest, will openly be taught and practiced, the air will be rent with the cries and distress, the soil soaked with blood, and the nation black with crimes."*

In his book *Why We're Polarized*, Ezra Klein says that today American polarization goes beyond just partisan politics. Our political identity includes cultural choices such as the food we eat, where we shop, even what movies and TV shows we prefer.

> *When you vote for a candidate you're not just voting for him or her. You are voting for, well, everything...You're voting for your side to beat the other side. You're voting to express your identity....You're voting so those smug jerks you fight with in comment sections don't win, so that aunt or uncle you argue with at Thanksgiving can't lord it over you. You're voting to say your group is right and worthy and the other group is wrong and unworthy. That's bigger than any one candidate for president.*

An organization called **More in Common** has a project to study polarization and learn what can be done to bring people together. In a report entitled "Hidden Tribes: A Study of America's Polarized Landscape," their researchers conclude that the majority of Americans are really tired of the divisiveness and actually do share a common set of beliefs.

> *A majority of Americans, whom we've called the "Exhausted Majority," are fed up by America's polarization. They know we have more in common than that which divides us: our belief in freedom, equality, and the pursuit of the American dream.*

After analyzing over 200,000 pieces of information and surveying 8,000 Americans, they conclude that this is the heart of the American identity:

> *To be American, for most, does not require someone to be white or to be Christian. Rather it is to believe in freedom and equality, and to pursue the American Dream.*

This study confirms that these are indeed our core American values.

Where did these American values come from? And how have they endured since the founding of our nation?

1. We have to take a look back at our history.

2. We have to examine our deep-seated *cultural values* of freedom, equality of opportunity, and the pursuit of the American Dream— achieving a better life for ourselves and our families, according to our personal definition of success.

3. We have to understand how the founders conceived a government that was of the people, by the people, and for the people— envisioning a land where all could be treated equally; the freedom of the individual was protected; and the role of government was limited.

4. We have to acknowledge that these are *ideals* that we strive for— *aspirational goals* imperfectly realized. From the beginning of our history, there have been glaring failures to live up to these ideals.

Throughout our discussion of core values, we will be drawing on the wisdom of a famous observer of the American scene, Alexis de Tocqueville.

- Tocqueville came to the United States as a young Frenchman in 1831 to study the American form of democracy and what it might mean to the rest of the world.

- After a visit of only nine months, he wrote a remarkable book called *Democracy in America,* considered a classic study of the American way of life.

- He described not only the democratic system of government and how it operated, but also its effect on how Americans think, feel, and act.

- It had been only about forty years since the adoption of the U.S. Constitution, but the new form of government had already produced a society of people with unique values.

- Tocqueville had unusual powers of observation. Many scholars believe that Tocqueville had a deeper understanding of traditional

American beliefs and values than anyone else who has written about the United States.

- What is so remarkable is that many of these traits of the American character, which he observed nearly 200 years ago, are still visible and meaningful today.

What are the American values and beliefs that Tocqueville observed? Are they the same as the ones recently identified by the More in Common survey—freedom, equality, and the pursuit of the American Dream?

Are these values the basis of our American identity? Do we have a common identity that transcends polarization?

Who are we? Let's take a closer look.

Question: How would you describe who we are?

SOURCES

https://theconversation.com/pessimists-have-been-saying-america-is-going-to-hell-for-more-than-200-years-145662

https://facingtoday.facinghistory.org/why-were-polarized-a-review-of-ezra-kleins-book

https://hiddentribes.us/

Democracy in America, by Alexis de Tocqueville, Specially Edited and Abridged for the Modern Reader by Richard D. Heffner, A Mentor Book Published by The New American Library. NY (1956)

Chapter 4

WHAT MAKES US "AMERICANS"?

Picture yourself sitting in the middle of the Moscow Symphony. You're a Russian cellist on tour in the United States, and you know that some of your fellow orchestra musicians are actually members of the KGB, watching you to make sure you don't "run away."

This was the story I heard back in the early 1970s from a friend who did manage to escape and defect to the United States.

The orchestra was on a world tour, and that night they were playing a concert in New York City. The KGB had them on a short leash—making sure they stayed in their hotel rooms and went to and from the concert hall as a group, never venturing out alone.

My friend told an exciting story about retrieving his cello before it was packed up, and then rushing to the subway to make his escape. He sat down in the train with a sigh of relief, but it did not leave for about five minutes. He was sure that at any moment the KGB would appear, but he made it and was soon united with his New York friends.

This musician also had friends in Japan and various European countries who had offered to help him defect, and he gave it much thought over several years. He could easily have chosen one of those other nations, in search of freedom.

"Why did you decide to come to the United States?" I asked.

"Because I would always be a foreigner in the other countries," he replied. "But here, I would fit in. I wouldn't be different—I would just be an American."

What is it about the United States that has allowed us to take in immigrants from all over the world and create new "Americans"?

The pollster John Zogby says that what holds the United States together is that *"we all share a common set of values that make us American.... We are defined by the rights we have.... Our rights are our history, why the first European settlers came here and why millions more have come here since."*

What are these shared rights that all Americans hold dear? *Freedom, equality of opportunity, and the pursuit of the American Dream.*

From the beginning, European settlers came here for freedom, and an equal chance for a better life. And this is why the "huddled masses yearning to breathe free" still come from all over the world.

Immigrants may wait years to enter legally or risk their lives trying to cross the border without legal status. The quest for freedom is at the heart of their desire to come to the United States—freedom to live their lives as they choose and have a shot at the American Dream, however they may define it.

But that is only part of the story. Historically there was work to be done to establish a new nation, a series of conditions to be met, responsibilities to fulfill—even prices to pay for these valuable rights that evolved into our unique cultural values system.

The experience of the first European settlers shaped our common set of cultural values:

- They came for freedom, but they had to be self-reliant to survive.

- They came for an equal opportunity to succeed, but they had to compete with others.

- They came for a better life, for themselves and their children, but they had to work hard to achieve it.

Essentially, they came for what we now call "the American Dream," but self-reliance, competition, and hard work were necessary to succeed.

We universally accept freedom, equality of opportunity and the American Dream as our American rights, but in some ways they must be earned. Over time, the accompanying responsibilities—self-reliance, competition, and hard work—have become important component parts of the cultural value system.

It is this immigrant experience (past and present) and a core set of values that define us as Americans—three reasons why people have come here, and still do—for freedom, equality of opportunity, and the American Dream, and three prices to be paid for these benefits—self-reliance, competition, and hard work.

We can visualize these six values as a **paradigm** consisting of **three pairs** of rights/benefits and responsibilities/prices to pay for these benefits:

Rights/Benefits	**Responsibilities/Prices to Pay**
Individual Freedom	Self-Reliance
Equality of Opportunity	Competition
The American Dream	Hard Work

Traditionally immigrants have come to the United States for freedom, an equal opportunity for success, and a chance for the American Dream. The dream of freedom and a better life for themselves and their families still draws immigrants today, and they are willing to pay the price for success.

1. People come for **Individual Freedom,** but the price for that is **Self-Reliance**. We cannot be truly free if we cannot take care of ourselves and be independent.

2. They expect **Equality of Opportunity**, but the price for that is **Competition**. If everyone has an equal *chance* for success, then we have to compete.

3. Their ultimate desire is **The American Dream**, the opportunity for a better life and a higher standard of living. The price for the American Dream has traditionally been **Hard Work**.

The relationship among these values—the rights and the responsibilities—defines the American Dream—*the belief that if people take responsibility for their lives and work hard, they will have the individual freedom to pursue their personal goals and a good opportunity to compete for success.*

This **paradigm** was first created by Edward Kearny and presented in an English as a Second Language textbook he and I co-authored with JoAnn Crandall: *American Ways: An Introduction to American Culture*, published by Pearson and now in its fourth edition. The purpose of *American Ways* is to explain basic American beliefs and motivations to people from other countries, exploring how our value system has traditionally affected our institutions and virtually all areas of our lives.

This simple **paradigm** explains the core traditional American beliefs—our unique American cultural values. Deep down inside, we all believe these precepts to one degree or another.

However, we must acknowledge that it was *white* European settlers who established the dominant culture and primarily white *men* who wrote the founding documents.

- In 1776, slavery was legal in all of the original 13 colonies, and many of the Founding Fathers even owned enslaved people. Forty-one of the 56 signers of the Declaration of Independence were slave owners.

- In the Declaration of Independence, the phrase "all men are created equal" did not apply to women, indigenous peoples, or enslaved African-Americans, first brought to America in 1619.

- In many ways, black Americans have lived in a parallel universe since then, separated from the white universe by enslavement, then by legal segregation and racial discrimination.

- Many African-Americans and members of other minorities are still striving to fully access and experience our cultural benefits of individual freedom, equality of opportunity, and the American Dream.

Think about what unites us as Americans as you read on. Together we will examine each of these basic *cultural values* in detail, tracing their history, discussing their current relevance, and considering what our "reasoned commitment" to these "values and principles" should be.

Question: What do you think is unique about Americans?

SOURCES

The Values Divide: American Politics and Culture in Transition, by John Kenneth White, Forward by John Zogby, Chatham House Publishers of Seven Bridges Press. NY (2003)

American Ways: An Introduction to American Culture Fourth Edition, by Maryanne Kearny Datesman, JoAnn Crandall, and Edward N. Kearny, Pearson Education, Inc. White Plains, NY (2014)

https://vintageamericanways.com/american-ways-book/

Chapter 5

THE LAND OF THE FREE

What is the number one reason why people want to immigrate to the United States?

It is probably for freedom—be it political, religious, economic, or some other personal reason.

I was discussing this with a friend whose grandparents had emigrated from Russia in the 1800s. I put forth my theory that most immigrants come for some type of freedom, but he was dubious. So I asked him what *he* thought drew people to the United States. What did he think was so unique about America, and he replied, "the rule of law." (He *is* an attorney, after all.)

Then several days later, he re-opened the conversation:

> *"I've been thinking about what you said about the value of freedom. That was why my grandparents came here—for freedom. They were Russian Jews experiencing religious persecution, and they literally fled for their lives. Freedom was something that my grandfather talked about often, but not so much my parents. Maybe that intense feeling about freedom wears off after several generations."*

Yes, maybe we do take freedom for granted and don't think about it much. Probably so, by the third generation. But our desire for individual freedom is deeply rooted in our history.

The earliest white settlers came to the North American continent to establish colonies that were free from the controls that existed in European societies. It was these white European settlers who established the dominant culture.

Ironically, they also bought African-American slaves here and systematically denied them their freedom for over 200 years.

What controls were the first European settlers fleeing?

They sought freedom from:

- kings and governments,

- priests and churches,

- noblemen and a hereditary aristocracy.

They wanted to escape the controls placed on many aspects of their lives, and to a great extent, they succeeded. In 1776, the British colonial settlers declared their independence from England and established a new nation, the United States of America. In so doing, they defied the king of England and declared that *the power to govern would lie in the hands of the people.*

They were now free from the power of the kings.

In 1787, when they wrote the Constitution for their new nation, they separated church and state so that there would never be a government-supported church.

This greatly limited the power of the church.

Also, in writing the Constitution they expressly forbade titles of nobility to ensure that an aristocratic society would not develop.

There would be no ruling class of noblemen in the new nation.

The historic decisions made by those first settlers have had a profound effect on the shaping of the American character.

- By limiting the power of the government and the churches and eliminating a formal aristocracy, the early settlers created a climate of freedom where the emphasis was on the individual.

- The United States came to be associated in their minds with the concept of individual freedom.

- This is probably the most basic of all the American values.

- Scholars and outside observers may call this value individualism, but most Americans use the word *freedom*. It is one of the most respected and popular words in the United States today.

- By freedom, Americans mean the desire and the right of all individuals to control their own destiny without outside interference from the government, a ruling noble class, the church, or any other organized authority.

The desire to be free of controls was a basic value of the new nation in 1776, and it has continued to attract immigrants to this country.

The colonial settlers came for various types of freedom:

- Some were escaping religious persecution.

- Some felt oppressed by European governments.

- Some felt trapped in a lower level of the social hierarchy of their country.

They wanted a fresh start. They were risk takers, ready to leave all the security of their native country for a chance of a better life in a "New World."

And they were determined to protect their individual freedoms.

However, we must again acknowledge how different the historical experience of black Americans has been. They did not choose to immigrate here; they were brought as enslaved persons, starting in 1619.

Slavery existed until after the bloody Civil War, and it was followed by the institutionalization of racism. This will be examined in greater detail in later chapters.

Question: Do you have any family stories about your ancestors coming to the United States? Were any of them seeking freedom?

SOURCES

https://vintageamericanways.com/american-values/

American Ways: An Introduction to American Culture Fourth Edition, by Maryanne Kearny Datesman, JoAnn Crandall, and Edward N. Kearny, Pearson Education, Inc. White Plains, NY (2014)

Chapter 6

COLONIAL HISTORY 101

Lin-Manuel Miranda's phenomenally popular Broadway hit "Alexander Hamilton" tells the story of Hamilton's role in the fight for American independence, the writing of the Constitution, and the first decades of the new nation.

- Hamilton greets the Frenchman Lafayette in 1781 at the battlefield of Yorktown, the final battle of the Revolutionary War.

- In the song "Yorktown (The World Turned Upside Down)," Hamilton—himself an immigrant—acknowledges Lafayette's help on the battlefield: "Immigrants—we get the job done!"

- The youngest of the "Founding Fathers," Hamilton argues for a strong central government at the Constitutional Convention, and writes 59 of the 85 Federalist Papers essays in support of ratifying the Constitution.

- Hamilton has a plan to assume the debts of the colonies and set up a national banking system.

- Madison and Jefferson meet over dinner with Hamilton and they agree to give him the power to create the financial system he envisions, in return for locating the capital on the Virginia-Maryland border.

- The song "The Room Where It Happens" describes the compromise between the two Virginians and "the immigrant." They enter the room as enemies but emerge with a compromise that satisfies both sides: the immigrant gains "unprecedented financial power," while the Virginians get the nation's capital. And no one really knows how the compromise is reached, "how the sausage gets made," because "no one else is in the room where it happens."

How did the colonists' strong desire for individual freedom lead to the establishment of a new country?

Time for a quick history refresher.

The 1500s and 1600s:

- Settlers came to America from different countries and set up colonies during the 1500s (Spain and France) and the 1600s (primarily Britain).

- A number of the British colonies were founded to protect specific religious groups from persecution.

- In 1607, the British Empire founded its first permanent colony in Jamestown, Virginia, and enslaved African-Americans were brought there in 1619.

- Massachusetts, New Hampshire, Maryland, Connecticut, Rhode Island, Delaware, North Carolina, South Carolina, New Jersey, New York, and Pennsylvania were all founded during the 1600s.

- Georgia was the last of the original 13 British colonies, founded in 1732.

The 1700s:

- By 1770, the colonists were chafing under British rule, complaining that they did not have the same rights as other British citizens.

- The cry was that they were subject to "taxation without representation."

- That year, a demonstration in Boston turned violent and British troops fired into the crowd—it became known as the "Boston Massacre."

- In 1773, there was the "Boston Tea Party," when rebellious colonists dumped tea from British ships into the harbor, protesting British taxation.

- In 1774, the fighting started in earnest with the "Battle of Bunker Hill" between the newly formed Continental Army and the British troops.

- In 1776, the colonists decided to band together and officially declare their independence from England.

- They were very specific about the rights they wanted to have.

What was the significance of the Declaration of Independence?

The colonists wanted to define the role of government and protect their individual rights.

- They specified three rights in the Declaration of Independence, July 4, 1776: life, liberty, and the pursuit of happiness.

- They asserted these are *God-given rights* and they cannot be taken away by government:

We hold these truths to be self-evident, that all men are created equal, that they are endowed by their Creator with certain unalienable Rights, that among these are Life, Liberty and the pursuit of Happiness.

— That to secure these rights, Governments are instituted among Men, deriving their just powers from the consent of the governed,

— That whenever any Form of Government becomes destructive of these ends, it is the Right of the People to alter or to abolish it, and to institute new Government, laying its foundation on such principles and organizing its powers in such form, as to them shall seem most likely to effect their Safety and Happiness.

(However, as mentioned before, these God-given rights did not apply to women, indigenous peoples, or enslaved African-Americans. More later about the paradox of slavery in a nation founded on liberty and equality.)

The British weren't about to let their profitable colonies go, so the colonists had to fight a Revolutionary War.

- The troops, led by George Washington, fought for six years, greatly aided by French soldiers and France's financial support.

- In 1781, the British began to withdraw, and the Treaty of Paris in 1783 officially ended the war.

The 13 colonies came together with a weak form of government, under the Articles of Confederation.

- There was only one government branch—Congress—and it had very little power.

- The 13 states each had their own individual Constitutions describing their state governments, and specifying the rights held by their citizens.

- The states were so heterogeneous that they operated much like a series of small, independent countries.

- How could they maintain their individual identities and differences without giving up precious freedom?

Finally, in 1787 a group of "Founding Fathers" came together in Philadelphia and wrote a new Constitution.

The trick was to create a form of government that was strong enough to hold the country together, while preventing the national government from taking too much power away from the states, or from individuals.

Question: What role does a government have in protecting the individual freedom of its citizens?

SOURCES

https://www.allmusicals.com/h/hamilton.htm

https://www.archives.gov/founding-docs/declaration-transcript

Chapter 7

WE THE PEOPLE: OUR UNIQUE CONSTITUTION

In George Orwell's *1984*, Big Brother watches people's every move from ubiquitous telescreens, and The Party exercises complete control over their lives. A Party leader explains:

> *The Party seeks power entirely for its own sake. We are not interested in the good of others; we are interested solely in power, pure power....*
>
> *The German Nazis and the Russian Communists came very close to us in their methods, but they never had the courage to recognize their own motives. They pretended, perhaps they even believed, that they had seized power unwillingly and for a limited time, and that just around the corner there lay a paradise where human beings would be free and equal.*
>
> *We are not like that.*
>
> *We know that no one ever seizes power with the intention of relinquishing it.*
>
> *Power is not a means; it is an end. One does not establish a dictatorship in order to safeguard a revolution; one makes the revolution in order to establish the dictatorship.*

What is so unique about the Constitution of the United States?

When it was written, there was nothing like it on the face of the earth.

- Tocqueville referred to it as "the most perfect federal constitution that ever existed."

- Historians have called it "this country's greatest gift to human freedom," because *for the first time, power was in the hands of the people, not the government.*

- The Constitution would protect the people from their government and it would specifically limit its power over their lives.

The writers of the Constitution were certainly influenced by previous documents such as the Magna Carta and the English Bill of Rights, as well as the writings of John Locke, Thomas Hobbes, and Montesquieu.

However, James Madison, the principal author of the Constitution, saw this one important difference between those documents and what was created for the United States:

In Europe, charters of liberty have been granted by power. America has set the example...of charters of power granted by liberty.

Freedom was not to be granted by the authority of the government.

Instead, the principles of liberty and *the will of the people* would determine *how much power the government would be allowed.*

The Preamble to the Constitution has the first three words written in very large letters to emphasize the power of the people:

WE THE PEOPLE of the United States, in order to form a more perfect union, establish justice, insure domestic tranquility, provide for the common defense, promote the general welfare, and secure the blessings of liberty to ourselves and our posterity, do ordain and establish this Constitution for the United States of America.

The Constitution established three branches of government—the executive, legislative, and judicial, with a system of checks and balances to divide the power and prevent one branch from dominating the other.

During the Constitutional Convention, the need to enumerate individual rights was hotly debated.

- The Federalists argued that it was not necessary to have a Bill of Rights; they believed the entire Constitution offered appropriate protections.

- But the Anti-Federalists wanted to make sure that the new government could never encroach on individual freedoms.

- Although state constitutions had individual rights specified, when the Federal Constitution was completed on September 17, 1787, it lacked any sort of Bill of Rights.

The new Constitution then had to be ratified by 9 of the 13 states. (Three-quarters of all states must ratify any change to the Constitution.)

- By 1788, the requisite 9 states had voted for ratification, but Virginia, New York, Rhode Island, and North Carolina had not, holding out for a Bill of Rights.

- James Madison promised the Virginia legislators that the Constitution would be amended upon its ratification, and they acquiesced, as did New York.

- The following year, in 1789, the first 10 Amendments—the Bill of Rights— were added and ratified.

The new country now had a new Constitution, with a Bill of Rights.

What rights and freedoms are specified in the Bill of Rights? (See Appendix for the exact wording and more of an explanation.)

1. Freedom of religion, speech, and the press; the right to peaceably assemble and petition the government about grievances
2. The right to bear arms ("A well regulated Militia, being necessary to the security of a free State, the right of the people to keep and bear Arms, shall not be infringed.")
3. Quartering of soldiers (limitations on soldiers being housed in private homes)
4. The right to be free from unreasonable search or arrest
5. Individual rights in criminal cases (not testifying against oneself; no double jeopardy)
6. The right to a fair trial in criminal cases (including speedy trial by jury, and right to a defense attorney)
7. Rights in civil cases
8. Bails, fines, and punishments (prohibits excessive bails, fines, and cruel or unusual punishment)
9. Rights retained by the people (even if not specifically enumerated)
10. States' rights (power not given to the Federal Government retained by states or the people)

Question: What do you think is the most important feature of the U.S. Constitution?

SOURCES

https://www.goodreads.com/quotes/5723-now-i-will-tell-you-the-answer-to-my-question

https://ari.aynrand.org/a-charter-of-power-granted-by-liberty/

https://constitutioncenter.org/media/files/constitution.pdf

https://www.archives.gov/files/legislative/resources/education/bill-of-rights/images/handout-3.pdf

"A Promise of Freedom" film by US Citizenship and Immigration Services. https://www.youtube.com/watch?v=so14G_BOPbI

Chapter 8

SELF-RELIANCE: THE PRICE FOR INDIVIDUAL FREEDOM

Jeff Bezos, founder of Amazon, says he owes his success in business to two traits he learned from his grandfather—self-reliance and resourcefulness.

> *"I spent all my summers on his ranch, from age 4 to 16, and [Jeff's grandfather, Pop] was incredibly self-reliant. You know, if you're in the middle of nowhere, in a rural area, you don't pick up the phone and call somebody when something breaks, you figure out how to fix it yourself.*
>
> *So, as a kid, I got to see him solve all these problems and be a real problem solver.... We learned a lot of things from watching him, because he would take on major projects that he didn't really know how to do and then figure out how to do them."*

Bezos explains how the resourcefulness and self-reliance he learned on his grandfather's ranch helped him in business:

> When you are trying to move things forward, you run into problems and have failures.
>
> When things don't work, you have to back up and try again.
>
> *"Each one of those times when you have to step back, back up, and try again. You're using resourcefulness, you're using self-reliance. You're trying to invent your way out of a box, and we have tons of examples at Amazon where we have had to do this. We failed so many times. I always think of us as a great place to fail because we're good at it. We have so much practice."*

Where did the American belief in self-reliance come from?

From the beginning, self-reliance has always been a strong trait among immigrants to the United States.

- Going back to the 1600s, independence and resourcefulness were critically important.

- The very lives of the early settlers depended on their ability to take care of themselves and their families.

- The first settlers left everything behind to start a new life in a new land.
- They had to build houses, find food, create a workable government, and eventually fashion a whole new nation.
- They came for freedom but had to be self-reliant in order to survive.
- In time, self-reliance itself became a cultural value.
- It was greatly strengthened by the settling of the American frontier, from 1790 to 1890.

By the 1830s, Tocqueville observed this American belief in action:

They owe nothing to any man, they expect nothing from any man; they acquire the habit of always considering themselves as standing alone, and they are apt to imagine that their whole destiny is in their own hands.

What is the impact of the American cultural value of self-reliance?

It is no surprise that Bezos learned resourcefulness from his grandfather working on a ranch in the West.

- Bezos says that the ranch was "out in the middle of nowhere, in a rural area" where you had to be independent.
- The West is strongly associated with the frontier experience and the trait of self-reliance.
- Many Americans find the image of pioneer life inspiring, even though it has been greatly mythologized and largely ignores the horrific, shameful treatment of the native American Indians.
  - The U.S. government broke every treaty it made with the indigenous people.
  - In the 1830s, for example, when gold was discovered on Cherokee land in Georgia, the U.S. government forcibly evacuated the native Americans and marched them to relocate in Oklahoma. One in four of the Cherokee died on the 800-mile march known as The Trail of Tears.
- Nevertheless, today there is still a certain romanticized nostalgia for the old West as a simpler time, where people didn't need help from the government or any other institution, and self-reliance reigned supreme.

There are three traits that were shaped by the value of self-reliance:

- Inventiveness

- The "Can-Do" spirit of problem solving
- Basic optimism about the future

The need for self-reliance on the frontier encouraged a spirit of inventiveness, problem-solving, and optimism.

- Frontier men and women not only had to provide most of their daily life essentials, but they were also constantly facing new problems and situations that demanded innovative solutions.

- The willingness to experiment and invent led to another American trait, a "can-do" spirit, or a sense of optimism that every problem has a solution.

- Americans like to believe that a difficult problem can be solved immediately—an impossible one may take a little longer, taking pride in meeting challenges and overcoming difficult obstacles.

- In the 1830s, Tocqueville observed that no other country in the world "more confidently seizes the future" than the United States.

- Traditionally, when times are hard, political leaders have reminded Americans of the tough determination of their pioneer ancestors.

The American can-do spirit is still a source of pride, inspiration, and optimism.

Question: When is it important to be self-reliant?

SOURCES

https://www.inc.com/peter-economy/jeff-bezos-just-revealed-shocking-event-that-made-him-self-reliant-wildly-successful.html

https://www.cnbc.com/2019/05/01/amazon-billionaire-jeff-bezos-on-the-2-greatest-life-lessons-he-learned-from-pop.html

https://www.cnbc.com/2020/07/08/how-jeff-bezos-experience-working-on-farm-as-a-kid-shaped-amazon.html

https://www.pbs.org/newshour/show/why-native-americans-are-buying-back-land-that-was-stolen-from-them

These Truths: A History of the United States, by Jill Lepore, W. W. Norton & Company, NY (2018)

American Ways: An Introduction to American Culture Fourth Edition, by Maryanne Kearny Datesman, JoAnn Crandall, and Edward N. Kearny, Pearson Education, Inc. White Plains, NY (2014)

Chapter 9

EQUALITY OF OPPORTUNITY: A MIGHTY ASPIRATION

Thomas Peterffy arrived in the United States in December of 1965, with a single suitcase containing a change of clothes, his slide rule, and a handbook on surveying. He was 20 years old, fleeing communist oppression in Hungary. He did not speak any English and he did not have any money.

According to an article in *Forbes* magazine, Peterffy sought refuge in a Hungarian community in Spanish Harlem:

> *"It was a big deal to leave home and my culture and my language," he says. "But I believed that in America, I could truly reap what I sowed and that the measure of a man was his ability and determination to succeed. This was the land of boundless opportunity."*

Peterffy worked his way up from a job in a surveying firm to founding his own company in the 1970s. He was a pioneer in creating ways to conduct stock trades electronically, even before the digitization of the markets. In the 1990s, he founded the Interactive Brokers Group and at age 72, his financial worth was estimated at $12.6 billion.

Clearly, the United States did prove to be the land of boundless opportunity for Peterffy, as it has for numerous other immigrant entrepreneurs.

Forty-two of the Forbes 400 Richest People in America are naturalized citizens who immigrated to this country, and half of the American tech companies worth $1 billion or more were founded by immigrants.

How did Equality of Opportunity become an important American cultural value?

From the beginning, America was known as "the land of opportunity," where people could achieve anything they put their mind to, no matter who they were (assuming they were white). All the ingredients were there:

- Incredible natural resources: a multitude of trees, rich fertile farmland, wild game, an extensive system of rivers, and an agreeable climate

- Relatively few Native Americans living on this land, with neither the weapons nor the organization to keep the European settlers out, and little resistance to the diseases they brought with them

- No strong government or church to limit their freedom, no social structure that proscribed the parameters of their future lives

Freedom and economic opportunities flourished, and the colonies evolved. When the colonists decided to band together and create a new country in 1776, they faced a challenge: How could they ensure that the land of opportunity would also be a land of *equality* of opportunity for *all* (white, male) Americans?

- The Declaration of Independence articulated the national value of equality: *"We hold these truths to be self-evident, that all men are created equal..."*

- In 1789, the Constitution limited the powers of the government, protected individual freedoms, and gave citizens equal opportunities to succeed.

- Because titles of nobility were expressly forbidden in the Constitution, no formal class system developed in the United States.

Immigrants had a better chance for personal success without a hereditary aristocracy, and other political and religious controls.

For the next hundred years (1790 to 1890), the settling of the western territories reinforced the cultural value of equality of opportunity:

- On the frontier, people treated each other more as social equals than in the settled eastern regions of the country.

- Because so little attention was paid to a person's family background, the frontier offered a new beginning for many Americans who were seeking opportunities to advance themselves.

- Opportunities were plentiful on the frontier. There was a continuous need for new settlers: farmers, skilled laborers, merchants, lawyers, and political leaders.

- There were fewer differences in wealth on the frontier than in the eastern states; frontier Americans lived, dressed, and acted more alike, whether rich or poor.

By the 1830s, Tocqueville could see equality of opportunity at work on the frontier. He observed:

> *The more I advanced in the study of American society, the more I perceived that...equality of condition is the fundamental fact from which all others seem to be derived.*

What is the state of equality of opportunity today?

Today, over 90 percent of Americans believe that equality of opportunity is an "absolutely essential" American ideal—according to Stanford University. But what does that mean?

- Most Americans believe **everyone should have an equal** *chance* **for success—not that all people should actually be equal.** This is an important distinction.

- We must recognize that equality of opportunity is (and has always been) an *ideal*—a mighty *aspiration*, not always achieved.

- While it continued to develop as an American ideal through the 1800s, sizable portions of the population were excluded: African-Americans, women, and Native Americans. Their *legal* access to the right of equality of opportunity was delayed until well into the 20th century.

- We are still working to make the *aspiration* of equality of opportunity a *reality* for all.

Question: What does equality of opportunity mean to you?

SOURCES

https://www.forbes.com/sites/monteburke/2016/10/04/6-immigrant-stories-that-will-make-you-believe-in-the-american-dream-again/#6f517daf8027

https://edeq.stanford.edu/about/overview

American Ways: An Introduction to American Culture Fourth Edition, by Maryanne Kearny Datesman, JoAnn Crandall, and Edward N. Kearny, Pearson Education, Inc. White Plains, NY (2014)

Chapter 10

EQUALITY OF OPPORTUNITY: A VEXING PARADOX

How do we reconcile the ideal of equality of opportunity with slavery?

In order to rationalize the existence of slavery in "the land of the free," there was a continuing attempt to de-humanize enslaved African-American people—often tearing families apart when selling them as property.

Enslaved African-Americans were not only considered as *inferior* to whites, they were thought to *lack emotional ties to their family members, and be incapable of parental love.*

There is a poignant moment in *The Adventures of Huckleberry Finn*, where Huck realizes that this is not true. While floating down the river, Huck hears his slave friend Jim crying in the night. Jim spends his night watches "moaning and mourning" for his wife and two children.

Though "it don't seem natural," Huck concludes that Jim loves his family as much as white men love theirs:

> *When I waked up just at daybreak he was sitting there with his head down betwixt his knees, moaning and mourning to himself. I didn't take notice nor let on. I knowed what it was about. He was thinking about his wife and his children, away up yonder, and he was low and homesick; because he hadn't ever been away from home before in his life; and I do believe he cared just as much for his people as white folks does for their'n. It don't seem natural, but I reckon it's so.*

It is this moment when Huck's perspective on slavery and society's hypocritical, cruel principles shifts; he will *not* return Jim to his owner, even if it means breaking the law.

Huck rips up his letter to Jim's owner, declaring that he'd rather be damned than defy his gut instinct; "I'll go to hell," he says.

When did enslavement begin and end in the United States?

Here are some historical highlights:

- Slavery existed in colonial times; the first enslaved Africans were brought here in 1619.

- By 1776, there were enslaved people in all 13 colonies.
- 20-25% of the population of Boston and Newport were slaves.
- 40% of the population of Virginia were slaves, and 60% of South Carolina.
- The founding fathers debated the problem of slavery and chose to leave it to the states to decide.
- In the Constitution, enslaved individuals were counted as three-fifths of a person.
- The Constitution stipulated that no new slaves could be brought into the United States after 1808.
- Slavery was gradually phased out in the North and had ended in all northern states by 1804.
- Enslavement continued in the southern states and a number of western territories.
- Although no new slaves were imported, their total number increased from almost 700,000 in the first census of 1790 to almost *4 million* in 1860, as succeeding generations were born into slavery.
- It took a terrible, bloody Civil War (1861-1865) and a Constitutional amendment (1865) to finally end enslavement throughout the United States.

What a tragic paradox. In the 1830s Tocqueville had observed the great equality of the American society at large, but he also predicted trouble between blacks and whites:

These two races are fastened to each other without intermingling; and they are unable to separate entirely or to combine. Although the law may abolish slavery, God alone can obliterate the traces of its existence.

Slavery created a parallel universe in the United States, where the two races were separate and unequal although they lived side by side. African-Americans suffered terrible inequalities in a country founded on the ideals of freedom and equality of opportunity, rights enjoyed by white males.

Indeed, while the cultural values were being forged in the new nation, *the practice of enslavement denied African-Americans every single one of the country's benefits: freedom, equality of opportunity, and the pursuit of the American Dream—the chance to create a better life for their children.*

Enslavement also denied blacks opportunities to earn these rights—through self-reliance, competition, and hard work. Their subjugation prohibited them from being independent, and their hard work benefited the slave owner, not their own families.

What happened after slavery ended?

The legacy of slavery continued after the 13th Amendment had outlawed enslavement throughout the United States, in December, 1865.

In 1868 the 14th Amendment gave citizenship and equal protection under the law to all people born or naturalized in the United States, and *the right to vote to all males 21 years of age*, technically giving African-Americans the right to vote.

In 1870 the 15th Amendment *specified that African-Americans had the right to vote:* "The right of citizens of the United States to vote shall not be denied or abridged by the United States or any state on account of race, color, or previous condition of servitude."

The South immediately began efforts to take away these voter rights through "black codes," intimidation, and voter suppression laws.

- By the 1890s segregation laws were being passed, along with regulations designed to prohibit blacks from voting.

- Some laws required potential voters to own property, a virtual disqualifier for former slaves, most of whom never received the "forty acres and a mule," promised during the Reconstruction.

- Other laws required voters to pass literacy tests.

- Laws forbidding slaves from learning to read and write had resulted in widespread illiteracy, with almost one-third of all adult African-American males still unable to read or write 50 years later.

- The Plessy v. Ferguson Supreme Court decision in 1896 ruled that states could constitutionally pass laws segregating blacks and whites as long as the separate facilities were equal.

- Ninety percent of African-Americans lived in the South, so southern segregation and voter-suppression laws had produced an almost complete disenfranchisement of black voters by 1910.

Conditions in the southern state of Louisiana illustrate just how complete this disenfranchisement was.

- In 1896, more than 130,000 African-Americans were registered to vote.

- By 1904 there were 1,342.

- By 1910, even though blacks made up almost fifty percent of Louisiana's population, there were only 730 blacks registered to vote in the entire state, less than one percent of eligible African-American male voters.

In 1920, the 19th Amendment gave women the right to vote everywhere in the United States, but African-Americans had to wait another 40 years for laws to protect their rights.

The Civil Rights Act of 1964 was passed to end segregation in public places and prohibit employment discrimination on the basis of race, color, religion, sex, or national origin.

The Voting Rights Act of 1965 was passed to enforce 15th Amendment voting rights and prohibit racial discrimination at the polls.

What is the importance of our ideals?

From the beginning, the ideal of equality of opportunity has been just that—an American *ideal*, an *aspiration*—a goal we seek for our nation.

There is evidence that the terrible legacy of slavery continues today. African-Americans sometimes still face both implicit and explicit discrimination in the United States, a century and a half after enslavement was ended. More on this later.

But here's the important point to remember: the United States *stands for* freedom and equality of opportunity for all. Do we have perfect freedom and equality of opportunity for all? No, we are still striving to meet these ideals. But our government was designed to give us a way to pass laws and even change the Constitution to extend these rights to all Americans.

We are still very much a work in progress. But the *ideal* of equality of opportunity for all Americans continues to be an important value.

We still believe that everyone *should* have an equal *chance* to succeed.

Question: What do you think is the state of equality of opportunity in the United States today?

SOURCES

https://www.sparknotes.com/nofear/lit/huckfinn/chapter-23/page_3/

https://www.memphislibrary.org/memphislibrary/wp-content/uploads/A-BRIEF-HISTORY-OF-SLAVERY-IN-AMERICA.pdf

https://en.wikipedia.org/wiki/Slavery_in_the_United_States

https://en.wikipedia.org/wiki/Slavery_in_the_United_States#/media/File:US_Slave_Free_1789-1861.gif

https://www.history.com/topics/black-history/slavery

https://vintageamericanways.com/whos-gran-daddy-origin-grandfather-clause/

https://www.scencyclopedia.org/sce/entries/slavery/

Chapter 11

COMPETITION: THE PRICE FOR EQUALITY OF OPPORTUNITY

Shahid Khan, the owner of the Jacksonville Jaguars, immigrated from Pakistan to the United States as a young man with $500 in his pocket and a dream of success in his heart.

"The U.S. was always the promised land for me," he says.

Khan enrolled as an undergraduate at the University of Illinois and supported himself by working nights as a dishwasher, earning $1.20 an hour.

"I was overjoyed. You just couldn't get a job like that where I came from," he says. *"My immediate thought was, 'Wow, I can work. I can be my own man. I control my destiny.'"*

According to *Forbes*, more than half of the richest tech companies in the United States have been founded by immigrants, who have traditionally dominated the entrepreneurial class.

Khan believes that the very act of immigrating is entrepreneurial, a self-selected risk taken in an effort to better one's circumstances. It's a mind-set.

"You leave everything you have and get on a plane," he observes. *"You can handle change. You can handle risk. And you want to prove yourself."*

American immigrants appreciate the opportunities they have, Khan believes, but they know they can't count on anyone giving them a break—they have to make it themselves. They have to compete.

Where did the cultural value of competition come from?

Competition is the price Americans pay for the value of equality of opportunity. If everyone has an equal chance to succeed, then people have to compete for success.

- From the beginning, the colonists valued individual freedom and equality of opportunity and they were willing to compete for success.

- In the 1760s, when the British imposed new taxes on commerce and limits on self-government, the colonists rebelled.

- The Americans declared their independence from Britain in 1776 and limited the power of the Federal Government in the new Constitution (1789).

- Without significant government controls over the economy, the free enterprise system developed and flourished.

- In the century that followed (1790-1890), the western frontier experience strengthened not only the ideals of individual freedom, self-reliance, and equality of opportunity, but also the cultural value of competition.

In the 1860s, Abraham Lincoln described life as a competitive race:

We…wish to allow the humblest man an equal chance to get rich with everybody else. When one starts poor, as most do in the race of life, free society is such that he knows he can better his condition; he knows that there is no fixed condition of labor for his whole life.

The American West certainly provided opportunities to race for success:

- the California gold rush in 1848,

- the Nevada silver rush of 1858,

- and the 1889 rush to claim land in Oklahoma, when thousands of people literally raced into the territory in wagons or on horseback to claim a parcel of land.

The new nation was also ideal for the development of small businesses. Tocqueville observed in the 1830s that even farmers possessed a strong entrepreneurial spirit and many started their own small businesses to increase their income.

What is the impact of competition on American life today?

Business competition is seen by many as a positive force that strengthens freedom.

- Business is based on the free market ideal.

- In contrast to a government-controlled economic system, the marketplace provides choices—what businesses will produce and what consumers will buy.

- Businesses create wealth for the nation and economic opportunities for individuals.

It was not until the Great Depression of the 1930s that government began to regulate business and provide social services to individuals.

The debate over the power of the government and the role of the free market has been going on ever since.

Many believe that competition brings out the best in individuals.

- It challenges people to perform at the highest level possible.

- It causes them to make goals and strive to meet or surpass them.

- It prevents complacency. When he ran Microsoft, Bill Gates observed, "Whether it's Google or Apple or free software, we've got some fantastic competitors and it keeps us on our toes."

- Competition focuses energy, increases activity level, and motivates people to get things done.

- Competition is a societal value. American children have traditionally been taught to compete in school and in sports from a young age.

- Playing team sports teaches discipline, teamwork, the importance of following rules, and fair play.

In an article in "Collegiate Times," Amanda Fields writes about learning the value of competition:

> *"Sports teach kids important values that they can carry through any challenge in life, such as discipline, time management, work ethic, aggression, competitive edge, attitude and strength. Many parents wonder how to instill these values into their children — my parents aimed to do so by signing me up for soccer. I played soccer from the age of four until my senior year of high school....*
>
> *Many kids today are told that they are special, without doing anything worthy of praise. When playing a competitive sport, you are beaten down and come back stronger. You learn that the criticism is for your own good.... The criticism instills a work ethic within a child without them knowing....*
>
> *In today's climate, children need sports more than ever. Kids need someone to tell them they aren't doing their best. They need someone to push them beyond their limits. They need to be taught hard work. In a society that is built on competition, competitive sports teach kids how to be successful with a positive attitude."*

Not everyone agrees that unfettered competition is in the best interest of the nation or for us as individuals. We'll take a look at the related role of government regulation later.

Question: What role do you think competition should play in our lives?

SOURCES

https://www.forbes.com/sites/monteburke/2016/10/04/6-immigrant-stories-that-will-make-you-believe-in-the-american-dream-again/#6f517daf8027

American Ways: An Introduction to American Culture Fourth Edition, by Maryanne Kearny Datesman, JoAnn Crandall, and Edward N. Kearny, Pearson Education, Inc. White Plains, NY (2014)

https://www.inc.com/peter-economy/20-brilliant-quotes-on-competition-from-highly-successful-business-leaders.html

http://www.collegiatetimes.com/opinion/more-than-a-participation-trophy-the-importance-of-competition-in-sports/article_374b3654-028f-11e7-93e5-1b276e3c5346.html

Chapter 12

THE AMERICAN DREAM: ILLUSION OR REALITY?

In 1987, the day before his 19th birthday, Alfredo Quinones-Hinojosa crawled up an 18' fence on the Mexican border, cleared the barbed wire, and leapt into California. Spurred by the dream of making enough money to buy food for his family back home, he had $65 in his pocket, and fierce determination in his soul.

The border patrol caught him and sent him back, but an hour later he returned to the same spot, and this time he made it.

"I've never been one who declines adventure," he says.

Today Quinones-Hinojosa, affectionately known as "Dr. Q," is one of the top brain surgeons in the United States.

Dr. Q went from undocumented Mexican immigrant to migrant farm worker and railroad welder, community college student, Harvard Medical School graduate, and then neurosurgeon at Johns Hopkins Medicine. He is now chair of Neurologic Surgery at Mayo Clinic in Jacksonville, Florida, researching a cure for brain cancer.

What drew Quinones-Hinojosa to the United States was the chance to escape poverty.

Short visits to California's San Joaquin Valley, where Quinones-Hinojosa's uncle Fausto was a foreman at a ranch, gave Quinones-Hinojosa a glimpse into the United States—and the American dream. At age 14, he spent two months there pulling weeds, making money to bring back to his family.

"That hard-earned cash proved that people like me were not helpless or powerless," he wrote.

"No one can take away your dreams," he said.

What drew Dr. Q to the United States was the chance for the American Dream.

What is the American Dream?

Ask Americans to define it, and you'll probably get a variety of answers.

- It means that everybody has the chance to get rich.

- It means having a good life for you and your family.

- It's the freedom to follow your own individual dreams of success.
- It's having your own home.
- It's your right to get an education and better your circumstances.
- It's your freedom to be who you want to be and live your life the way you want.

Others might argue the American Dream really doesn't exist anymore, especially for the middle class. More on that later.

Oxford Languages (Google's dictionary) defines the American dream as "the ideal by which equality of opportunity is available to any American, allowing the highest aspirations and goals to be achieved."

- The traditional meaning of the American Dream is the belief that everyone has the right and the opportunity to create a better life for themselves and their children.
- Some may use material measures to define the American Dream, but it is much more than that.
- It is a profound and dynamic force at the core of who we are. It is the manifestation of our individual freedom.

Where did the American Dream come from?

In a way, the American Dream was probably in the DNA of the first white settlers who came to North America, and subsequently in the immigrants who followed. Certainly the Founding Fathers were believers.

- Some authorities point to the Declaration of Independence as the foundation of the American Dream—the assertion that "the pursuit of happiness" is a God-given right!
- The Constitution spelled out individual rights and guaranteed that any power not specifically granted to the government must remain in the hands of the states, *or the people.*
- By the 1830s, the expectation of having a better life was evident. Alexis de Tocqueville referred to it as "the charm of anticipation," the result of 200 years of history.

From the 1790s through the 1800s, the abundance of the North American continent and the expansion into the western territories allowed the American Dream to become a reality for many in the new nation, with tragic exceptions.

The dream was deferred for African-American slaves, women, and Native Americans until well into the 20th century. Moreover, at various times, certain immigrant groups have been denied access to the American Dream—most notably the Chinese in the 1800s.

What is the impact of the American Dream today?

Jim Cullen, author of *The American Dream: A Short History of an Idea that Shaped a Nation*, says the concept is "deeply embedded in the nation's psyche." He writes,

> *It's a compelling message political leaders call on when the nation is in crisis, reminding Americans of their can-do experience, that individuals have the power to bring about change.*
>
> *Perhaps it's no coincidence that historian James Truslow Adams coined the phrase "American dream" during the depths of the Great Depression.*

The Coronavirus Pandemic of the 2020s raised questions about the viability of the American Dream.

- When it struck, the economy of the United States was booming by many measures. Although not everyone was enjoying prosperity, unemployment was at a historic low.

- Belief in the financial reality of the American Dream was solid, with polls showing a high degree of satisfaction among individual citizens.

- Michael R. Strain, a conservative economist, argued that upward mobility was still a documented force in America. Just as the virus was hitting the United States, his new book was published—*The American Dream is Not Dead (But Populism Could Kill It)*.

- However, according to the Federal Reserve, before the virus struck, almost 40% of Americans would have been unable to cover a $400 emergency expense and pay it off quickly.

- Currently, nearly 70% of Americans have less than $1000 in savings, and 45% have nothing saved at all!

- Income inequality has never been worse, with middle-income families holding only 17% of American wealth, and one in four babies now born below the poverty line.

- The economic downturn caused by the pandemic disproportionately affected minority and low-income workers, many of whom are paid as hourly employees without healthcare benefits.

In an article "Why The American Dream May Be Another Casualty Of The Coronavirus Pandemic," Steven Kraus reports on a survey he conducted with QuestionPro Consumer Pulse during the summer of 2020.

Kraus says that half of the adults surveyed described themselves as "more worried about my personal finances than ever before."

- According to the survey, about two-thirds of Americans now believe the American Dream has become very difficult for most people to achieve.

- Only one in three now believe in a fundamental tenet of the American Dream—that "young people today will be better off than their parents' generation."

So, what will be the effect of this latest economic crisis on the American Dream?

Is the dream dependent on a good economy, or is it an independent force that endures through good and bad times, an inspiring *ideal*, one of our three core beliefs—freedom, equality of opportunity, and the pursuit of the American Dream?

Question: What is the American Dream for you?

SOURCES

https://www.cnn.com/2013/05/24/health/lifeswork-dr-q/index.html

https://www.firstcoastnews.com/article/news/local/local-brain-surgeons-life-to-be-made-into-movie-by-brad-pitts-production-company/77-412623157

https://www.investopedia.com/terms/a/american-dream.asp

http://americanradioworks.publicradio.org/features/americandream/a1.html

The American Dream is Not Dead (But Populism Could Kill It), by Michael R. Strain, Templeton Press, West Conshohocken, PA. (2020)

https://www.nytimes.com/interactive/2021/07/12/opinion/covid-fed-qe-inequality.html

https://abcnews.go.com/US/10-americans-struggle-cover-400-emergency-expense-federal/story?id=63253846

https://www.minneapolisfed.org/article/2021/what-a-400-dollar-emergency-expense-tells-us-about-the-economy

https://www.fool.com/retirement/2019/12/18/the-percentage-of-americans-with-less-than-1000-in/

https://www.washingtonpost.com/opinions/2021/07/16/us-is-growing-more-unequal-thats-harmful-fixable/

https://www.childrensdefense.org/state-of-americas-children/soac-2021-income-inequality/

https://www.pewresearch.org/social-trends/2020/01/09/trends-in-income-and-wealth-inequality/

https://www.vox.com/2014/7/9/5881041/two-charts-that-show-americas-poverty-problems-start-at-birth

Stephen Kraus QuestionPro Survey https://img1.wsimg.com/blobby/go/8189d9db-6f72-4678-88e9-93d177ef0deb/downloads/Kraus%20QuestionPro%20Aug%202020.pdf?ver=1626653304574

https://stephenkraus.com/kraus%2Fquestionpro-8%2F20

Chapter 13

HARD WORK: THE PRICE FOR THE AMERICAN DREAM

Do Wan Chang and his wife Jin Sook came to the United States in 1981 with almost nothing. Martial law had recently been lifted from South Korea when they arrived in Los Angeles on a Saturday with "little more than a high school education."

Chang immediately scoured newspaper job listings, interviewed with a local coffee shop and by Monday was washing dishes and prepping meals on the morning shift.

"I was making minimum wage. ... It wasn't enough to get by."

So he tacked on eight hours a day at a gas station and on top of that started a small office-cleaning business that kept him busy until midnight. Jin Sook worked as a hairdresser.

While he was working at the service station, Chang noticed that the men in the garment business drove nice cars, and he decided to get a job in a clothing store.

In three years he and his wife were able to save enough money to open their own clothing store, eventually establishing a successful chain called Forever 21.

Their hard work paid off and today they are worth $3 billion.

This is the classic story of the American Dream—"going from rags to riches," through hard work and perseverance.

How did Hard Work become an important American value?

In the spring of 1609 after a terrible winter, John Smith the leader of the Jamestown colony exhorted all the settlers to work harder: "He that will not work, shall not eat."

From the beginning, hard work was essential to survival.

- The North American continent had vast, limitless natural resources, but the early settlers and later immigrants had to create everything—houses, clothing, a food supply, transportation, a system of government, and laws.

- After settlers had colonized the eastern coast in the 1600s and 1700s, they pushed forward into the western frontier and repeated the process in the 1800s.

Material wealth was seen as the just reward for hard work—the foundation of the American Dream.

- Without a hereditary aristocracy, the fortunes of the rich were not guaranteed by birth, and the poor were not condemned to remain in their low social position.

- Material wealth became the measure of success and social respect.

- In the late 1790s James Madison, the Father of the American Constitution, stated that the difference in material possessions reflected a difference in personal abilities.

- With such a fluid social structure and an abundance of economic opportunities, a person's wealth was not fixed. It could suddenly go lower as well as higher, motivating individuals to focus on accumulating material possessions.

In the 1830s, Tocqueville observed that all classes in American society thought about protecting their material possessions and looked for ways to acquire more.

- Tocqueville believed this was not greed, but insecurity, and that it was ultimately contributing to the wealth of the entire nation.

- He was impressed by the rapid progress made in such a short time in trading and manufacturing. The United States was already the world's second leading sea power and had constructed the longest railroads in the world.

- Tocqueville was concerned, however, about the effect of all this material success—making materialism into a value itself, rather than a means to an end.

Early on, materialism became entwined with religion, resulting in the "Protestant work ethic"—the belief in hard work and self-discipline in pursuit of material gain and other goals.

- Protestant leaders viewed the work of all people to be holy, not just that of priests.

- John Wesley, the leader of the Methodist faith, urged his followers to "Earn all you can, give all you can, save all you can."

- In 1900 Episcopal Bishop William Lawrence proclaimed, "Godliness is in league with riches…. Material prosperity is helping to make the national character sweeter, more joyous, more unselfish, more Christlike."

What value do Americans put on hard work now?

Americans may no longer think of their work as being holy, but they are certainly still influenced by the Protestant work ethic. Most believe that success is proportional to the amount of work expended.

A Cornell University study recently found that Americans on both the left and the right believe in hard work—effort determines success.

> *"This speaks to why we see so much value in American society placed on picking yourself up by your bootstraps to overcome any obstacle," said...author Christofer Skurka. "Notions of meritocracy and what is sometimes called the 'Protestant work ethic' are really interwoven into the American fabric, almost regardless of a person's political orientation."*

Another factor is that over the last generation many Americans have turned away from religion and toward work as a source of meaning in their lives.

In an essay in "The Atlantic," Derek Thompson replaces the term "Protestant work ethic" with something he calls "workism." He writes,

> *For the college-educated elite, work has morphed into a religious identity—promising transcendence and community, but failing to deliver.*
>
> *Today, elite American men have transformed themselves into the world's premier workaholics, toiling longer hours than both poor men in the U.S. and rich men in similarly rich countries.... Workism may have started with rich men, but the ethos is spreading—across gender and age.*

Thompson says that Millennials and American teenagers have bought into the belief that their work must be interesting, meaningful, and fulfilling, and they must not stop searching until they find a career that meets this definition.

Interestingly, the United States is the only rich country that does not have a single day of paid vacation mandated by the Federal Government, and the majority of Americans work more hours a year than workers in Western European countries.

Moreover, even those who are lucky to have paid vacation frequently don't take advantage of it, leaving about a third of their vacation days unused.

Here's an important question: given these views of work, what happens to the American psyche when a historical event such as the Coronavirus Pandemic takes away millions of jobs in the blink of an eye?

Question: What is the purpose of work?

SOURCES

https://www.forbes.com/sites/monteburke/2016/10/04/6-immigrant-stories-that-will-make-you-believe-in-the-american-dream-again/#6f517daf8027

https://en.wikipedia.org/wiki/He_who_does_not_work,_neither_shall_he_eat

American Ways: An Introduction to American Culture Fourth Edition, by Maryanne Kearny Datesman, JoAnn Crandall, and Edward N. Kearny, Pearson Education, Inc. White Plains, NY (2014)

https://phys.org/news/2019-08-left-americans-hard-success.html

https://www.theatlantic.com/ideas/archive/2019/02/religion-workism-making-americans-miserable/583441/

https://www.theatlantic.com/video/index/396521/future-work-in-america/

https://www.huffpost.com/entry/paid-vacation-in-the-us-america_l_5cfa5c70e4b06af8b5073ae6

Chapter 14

CULTURE WARS, AND RUMORS OF WARS: WHAT DIVIDES US NOW?

Several years ago, I heard a sad story.

A friend of mine, who had voted for Trump, told me she had actually lost her best friend of 30 years because of her vote!

I was incredulous. She stressed how close this relationship had been and how shocked she was when her friend said she didn't want anything more to do with her.

My friend had protested, "But I voted for Obama before—doesn't that count for something?" No, it did not. The other woman just couldn't get past that vote for Trump, and their friendship was over.

This is a dramatic illustration of the profound political fissures in the United States today.

Why are Americans so politically polarized now?

There is probably unanimous agreement that American politics are highly partisan, and the consensus is that it has gotten worse since the 2016 election.

But here's a surprise: A recent study by the Annenberg School for Communication "does not support this popular belief." Yphtach Lelkes led a research team that studied political polarization in 2014 and repeated the same study in 2016.

- *"I've been studying polarization for a long time," Lelkes says, "and elite discourse is arguably at its worst, which led us to theorize that partisanship would be worse since Trump took office. But we found that things really have not budged."*

- The study investigated how willing their participants were to "speak poorly of the other political party," and how they reacted to criticism of their own party.

- It also examined "the extent to which participants desired to avoid members of the opposite party, even when participating in activities that were not related to politics."

- The final aspect studied was "participants' willingness to commit or condone intentional actions designed to harm members of the opposing party."

Some believe that while President Obama emphasized American unity, President Trump sought to divide Americans. However, this study reveals that the country was already politically polarized back in 2014, and Trump's election in 2016 only revealed and exacerbated the chasm.

In the election of 2020, Biden ran on a vision of reuniting the country, but the nation remained stubbornly divided along party lines.

What is the root cause of this bitter political polarization?

In a nutshell, it is that *we can't agree about what the role of our government should be!*

- This is not a new argument—the Founders of our country had severe disagreements about how much power the Federal Government should have.

- John Adams and the Federalists advocated for a strong, centralized Federal Government, while Thomas Jefferson and the Anti-Federalists thought that the power of the national government should be limited.

- Jefferson believed that most of the governing power belonged at the state and local level.

The Declaration of Independence initially defined the role of government—to secure and protect our God-given rights of Life, Liberty and the pursuit of happiness.

> *We hold these truths to be self-evident, that all men are created equal, that they are endowed by their Creator with certain unalienable Rights, that among these are Life, Liberty and the pursuit of Happiness.*
>
> *— That to secure these rights, Governments are instituted among Men, deriving their just powers from the consent of the governed…*

However, the role of the government and the protection of our "God-given rights" is still a source of contention.

Ultimately, what should be the role of government in securing and protecting our rights?

The disagreement about what rights the government should guarantee has caused the "values divide" or the "culture wars" that began in the early 2000s.

- In *The Values Divide: American Politics and Culture in Transition,* John Kenneth White says that those on either side of the values divide live in "two parallel universes. Each side seeks to reinforce its thinking by associating with like-minded people."

- Those on the right and the left disagree strongly about the role of the government in solving the country's problems.

- Pew research documented this division in their study entitled "The Partisan Divide on Political Values Grows Even Wider."

- Among other questions, Pew survey participants chose between random pairs of statements about the government, indicating which one came closest to their beliefs—that "government regulation usually does more harm than good," or that "it is necessary to protect the public interest," for example.

The Coronavirus Pandemic brought this disagreement into clear focus. What should be the role of government in protecting the public health of the nation?

- Many on the left wanted the Federal Government to lead the fight against the virus—mobilizing industry to produce medical supplies and tests, setting national policies about shutting down public places to curb the spread, and mandating social distancing, the wearing of masks, and ultimately taking the COVID 19 vaccine.

- Many on the right rebelled against government regulations designed to control the virus and protect public health. Some openly defied rules about social distancing and wearing masks, considering such government measures a gross infringement on their personal freedom, particularly the requirement that their children wear masks in school. A few adamantly refused to take the vaccine, even if it meant losing their job.

How do people on the left and the right view the role of government in the context of our cultural values?

If we examine our paradigm for the American cultural values, most Americans would probably say they agree with the three rights or benefits—*everyone should have individual freedom, equality of opportunity, and the right to pursue the American Dream.*

The other side of the paradigm is where they may disagree—the responsibilities side, the price we may have to pay for these benefits. *Are self-reliance, competition, and hard work still part of the American value system?* Some would say that these values have fallen on hard times.

Those leaning liberal would probably say:

- Ideally Americans should eventually be self-reliant, but some people are so poor or badly disadvantaged that the government has a responsibility to reach down and give them a hand up.

- These individuals need help to get up to the starting line so they can compete on a level playing field. Eventually they will be able to work hard and hopefully achieve the American Dream.

Those leaning conservative would probably say:

- If the government gives the poor and disadvantaged too much help, it will enable them to be dependent—undermining the important values of self-reliance, competition, and hard work.

- Every American should have the right to individual freedom, equality of opportunity, and access to the American Dream—but they have the responsibility to "pull themselves up by their bootstraps" and work hard for their own success.

People of good will on both the right and the left want to see their government serve the needs of the American people. The debate over how exactly this should be accomplished started over 250 years ago and continues today.

Question: What do you think the role of government should be?

SOURCES

https://www.allsides.com/news/2019-10-17-1448/2016-election-did-not-increase-political-polarization

https://www.pewresearch.org/politics/2016/06/22/partisanship-and-political-animosity-in-2016/

https://www.archives.gov/founding-docs/declaration-transcript

The Values Divide: American Politics and Culture in Transition, by John Kenneth White, Forward by John Zogby, Chatham House Publishers of Seven Bridges Press. NY (2003)

https://www.pewresearch.org/politics/2017/10/05/the-partisan-divide-on-political-values-grows-even-wider/

https://www.pewresearch.org/politics/2018/04/26/the-public-the-political-system-and-american-democracy/

https://www.npr.org/2021/11/09/1053929419/feel-like-you-dont-fit-in-either-political-party-heres-why

Chapter 15

CHIPPING AWAY AT THE CULTURAL ICEBERG: WHAT UNITES US?

Back in 1978, I had the opportunity to visit Iran. A former English language student of mine, who had become a friend as we toiled over his doctoral dissertation, invited my husband and I to visit him and his family in Iran. The best part of our trip was not just seeing the magnificent sites of the country, but being entertained in Iranian homes in his native town of Jahrom, near Shiraz.

One day my friend took me to a neighboring town so he could confer with his uncle, who was now the head of the family. His uncle would tell him which of three teaching positions in different Iranian universities he should choose. The decision would be made on the basis of what would be best for the *family*, not what would be best for *him*.

This was so surprising to me.

Why was the welfare of his extended family more important than my friend's? If he had been married, I could have understood considering the opinions of his wife, but he was not. Why would he let his uncle decide his future?

The answer lies in the deep differences between our cultural values: Unlike Iran, in the United States we value the freedom of each individual family member to determine his or her own destiny.

Each family member should ultimately have an equal opportunity to seek his or her own version of the American Dream. It just seems like common sense, doesn't it?

But these deep-seated values of *individual freedom, equality of opportunity, and the right to pursue our individual dreams* are not universal. Just as different countries have different customs and lifestyles, they also have different deep-seated cultural values.

How can you define these deep cultural values of a diverse country like the United States?

Edward T. Hall, an anthropologist and expert in cross cultural communication, has summed up the challenge:

Culture hides much more than it reveals, and strangely enough, what it hides, it hides most effectively from its own participants.

> *Years of study have convinced me that the real job is not to understand foreign culture but to understand our own.*

Hall describes this phenomenon as the **cultural iceberg**, with the visible part above water representing the behavior of a culture (and some beliefs), and the much larger part under water as the deep-seated beliefs, values, and the thought patterns.

The vast majority of information about a culture is hidden, Hall says, and it is the hardest to understand.

- If we picture our country as an iceberg, the part above the water represents the *behavior* of Americans. You can observe what people are doing, even if you don't understand why. You may agree or disagree with what they're up to.

- At the surface of the water, or just below, are the *beliefs* of the people. Generally Americans can tell you what they believe about certain topics—off the top of their heads, or after some reflection.

- But it is the deep-seated *cultural values* that form the largest mass of the iceberg, invisible under the water. Generally, Americans are not able to articulate what these cultural values are.

- It is these hidden values that are the most interesting and the hardest to explain. They represent the internal—*even subconscious*—part of our culture that underlies and motivates the external, observable behavior.

This book focuses on the part of the cultural iceberg *below* the surface of the water—what it is about our culture that motivates us and causes such a diverse people to self-identify as "Americans," *our cultural values of freedom, equality of opportunity, the pursuit of the American Dream, self-reliance, competition, and hard work.*

How do our deep-seated cultural values operate?

It is important to remember several points about these values:

1. They are *cultural* values, *not moral or personal* values.

   - These American values are not taught explicitly; we learn them implicitly, and they form our "common sense" assumptions of how life should be.

   - They affect every aspect of our daily lives, consciously, or unconsciously.

   - These values are the cultural engine that powers the United States, creating a diverse nation of "Americans" composed of people from all over the world.

2. These values do not operate independently; they are part of an interconnected system.

   - Using a historical perspective, this framework of six basic traditional American values—freedom, self-reliance, equality of opportunity, competition, the American Dream, and hard work—has been described.

   - These cultural values operate in pairs, reflecting why people have come to America (and still do)—the benefits they seek and the price they pay to have these privileges.

     ○ Individual Freedom and Self-reliance
     ○ Equality of Opportunity and Competition
     ○ The American Dream and Hard Work

   - Putting these six values together into a system creates something new. As Aristotle said, the whole is greater than the sum of its parts.

   - The relationship among these values—the rights and the responsibilities—creates the fabric of the American society.

   - It is this fabric that defines the American Dream—*the belief that if people take responsibility for their lives and work hard, they will have the individual freedom to pursue their personal goals, and a good opportunity to compete for success.*

   - These six values are so tightly woven together that if any one of these threads is pulled out or even disturbed, the entire fabric is affected; it may even start to unravel. For example, some worry that if young people are unwilling to work hard, the benefits of freedom, equality of opportunity, and the pursuit of the American Dream may be endangered.

3. These cultural values are *ideals* that often do not reflect reality, but our unconscious belief in them defines who we are. We believe that Americans *should* all have an equal opportunity to succeed, in spite of demonstrable inequality in our society, for example.

   - Our cultural values determine our perception of the problems in our society and our decisions about how to solve them.

   - These ideals lie deep within our psyche. They tell us who we are as Americans, and what our country ultimately stands for.

   - They are *aspirational* values that inspire us and appeal to "our better angels." They often undergird our moral and personal beliefs, and are embraced in some degree by most Americans.

How do our shared values unite us?

Some worry that Americans are dividing themselves into tribes.

To listen to pundits and social media, one would definitely think so. In *Political Tribes: Group Instinct and the Fate of Nations*, Amy Chua observes that tribalism is part of human nature—the urge to be with others who are like ourselves.

However, Chua argues that America has become something more than a tribe. She defines it as

> *a super-group...a group in which membership is open to individuals of any background but that at the same time binds its members together with a strong, overarching, group-transcending collective identity,...a connection to the land, of being bound by a shared constitution.*

There truly is more that unites us than what divides us—even though these cultural bonds that tie us together may be largely unacknowledged or even unconscious.

America is more than just a sovereign nation—it is an idea, a noble experiment. As the pollster John Zogby observed, "We are defined by the rights we have."

Our history began with a quest for freedom, equality of opportunity, and the American Dream—creating a better life for ourselves and our families, and we forged a government that would protect these rights for ourselves and future generations:

> *WE THE PEOPLE of the United States, in order to form a more perfect union, establish justice, insure domestic tranquility, provide for the common defense, promote the general welfare, and secure the blessings of liberty to ourselves and our posterity, do ordain and establish this Constitution for the United States of America.*

This is who we are.

Question: What do you think unites this country?

SOURCES

https://www.spps.org/cms/lib/MN01910242/Centricity/Domain/125/iceberg_model_3.pdf

Beyond Culture, by Edward T. Hall, Anchor Books, NY (1976)

American Ways: An Introduction to American Culture Fourth Edition, by Maryanne Kearny Datesman, JoAnn Crandall, and Edward N. Kearny, Pearson Education, Inc. White Plains, NY (2014)

https://www.theatlantic.com/politics/archive/2018/05/amu-chua-tribalism/561662/

Political Tribes: Group Instinct and the Fate of Nations, by Amy Chua, Penguin Press, NY (2018)

https://constitutioncenter.org/media/files/constitution.pdf

Chapter 16

VALUES, BELIEFS, AND BEHAVIORS: "WE'RE ALL IN THIS TOGETHER."

It was a Thursday, the first day the airports reopened, and the planes started to fly again after 9/11. My husband and I drove to the nearly empty Reagan National Airport in Washington D.C. and boarded a plane for New York City.

Later that evening, we watched the sunset over what had been the twin towers of the World Trade Center. As it grew dark, two narrow shafts of white light rose from the site and extended high into the night sky, much higher than the physical towers had originally reached.

It was a profoundly moving moment.

Several days later, we were on a cruise ship waiting to cast off. There was another ship in the birth next to us, close enough to shout to the other passengers out on their balconies. After a few minutes, someone suddenly started to sing "God Bless America," and everyone on the two ships joined in.

It was another profoundly moving moment. We were one people, and we felt deep love for our country.

Initially, the Coronavirus Pandemic reminded us of how we felt during 9/11—*We're all in this together.*

- Other countries began to lockdown first. When we saw the empty streets of cities abroad, many wondered if Americans would ever voluntarily stay home, but during the March 2020 lockdown they did.

- In New York City, while Times Square was deserted, every night at 7:00 pm New Yorkers opened their windows, banged on pots and pans and cheered for the healthcare workers changing their shifts.

- People in small towns organized car parades and put green lights on their houses to honor our healthcare workers. In some neighborhoods, families stood in front of their houses to recite the Pledge of Allegiance every morning.

- Many felt a sense of patriotism. Instead of a foreign enemy, we were fighting a deadly virus, staying home to stop its spread—all of us making sacrifices for the common good.

However, after a few weeks the economy presented an even greater crisis—the stock market plummeted, schools were closed, and shuttered businesses began laying off workers. It wasn't too much longer before unity was supplanted by divisiveness. What happened?

What does our reaction to the Coronavirus Pandemic tell us about our cultural values, beliefs, and behaviors?

First of all, these three terms—**values, beliefs, and behaviors**—are being used in very specific ways. We often use the words "values" and "beliefs" interchangeably, but here they refer to two different concepts, as described by Hall's Cultural Iceberg.

- Our cultural *values* are in the hidden mass of the iceberg under the water, largely *unconscious* but a powerful influence on how we perceive and react to events: a core set of values that define us as Americans—three reasons why people have come here, and still do, and three prices to be paid for these benefits.

Rights/Benefits	Responsibilities/Prices to Pay
Individual Freedom	Self-Reliance
Equality of Opportunity	Competition
The American Dream	Hard Work

- Our *beliefs* are at—or just below—the water's surface, and they reveal our opinions and our judgments about what is true. These beliefs are the source of our national division, particularly our beliefs about our government: What is the true role of government in managing a national crisis such as the Coronavirus Pandemic?

- At the top of the iceberg, visible to all, are our *behaviors,* motivated by our deep cultural values, but filtered through our beliefs about how our government should serve our individual and collective needs. For example, during the pandemic, should we all wear masks, or not?

Second, if we look at the *behavior* of Americans during the pandemic—agreeing to wear masks or refusing to do so—we see these American *beliefs* and *values* at work.

- The controversy is an expression of two diametrically opposed *beliefs* about what the role of government should be. Should the government dictate our behavior to provide for the common good, even if it curbs our individual freedoms?

- However, at the *values* level, our deep-seated cultural values are still at play—freedom, equality of opportunity, and the American Dream.

What do we expect of our government in a crisis such as the pandemic?

After the lockdown ended, Americans were asked to wear masks when they left home. A man walked into the Post Office wearing his mask but was surprised to see that none of the other customers had one on. Only the postal workers behind the counter wore masks.

> When he reached the counter he inquired softly, "Why am I the only one wearing a mask?"
>
> The postal worker huffed, "Well, I wouldn't be wearing one either if I didn't have to. It's my constitutional right not to wear a mask!"

In a way, the virus stripped off a protective layer of civility, revealing profound emotional divisions in our beliefs about the proper role of government.

Many of those leaning liberal are strongly motivated by the value of *equality of opportunity*.

- The government should do more to address the problems of inequality revealed by the pandemic crisis—the virus disproportionately has affected Americans by race and class.

- There should be a healthcare system equally available to all and the government should guarantee healthcare as a basic human right.

- The government should put more money in the bank accounts of families and small "Mom and Pop" businesses and continue financial support during an economic crisis.

Many of those leaning conservative are more strongly motivated by the value of *individual freedom*.

- They are suspicious that temporary powers given to the government during an emergency may infringe on our basic rights and freedoms.

- They believe that government at any level should have limited power to proscribe or prevent public behavior.

- The government cannot tell them how to lead their lives—it cannot prevent them from operating or patronizing local businesses; it cannot force them to stay home or wear masks when they go out. And some actually quit their jobs when they were required to take the COVID 19 vaccination.

Where does this leave us?

Our deep-seated *cultural values* have been at work during the pandemic crisis, although we may have focused on our differing *behavior* and *beliefs*.

It is interesting to note that "cooperation" is not one of our six basic American *cultural values*. It is, however, an important *belief*.

When the pandemic began, neighbors reached out to each other, offering to get groceries or run errands for older Americans. Churches and other charitable organizations gathered non-perishables to stock food banks, and volunteers helped distribute supplies to those in need.

Our *cultural values* do not compel us to put the common good above individual freedom. However, our *moral and personal beliefs* often do so. Americans are some of the most caring, compassionate, generous people in the world. But helping and giving are individual choices, reflecting our cultural values of individual freedom and equality of opportunity.

If we look at the part of the iceberg visible above the water, we see *divisions in our behaviors brought on by differing beliefs*, particularly about the role of government. But this is only part of who we are.

We have to look below the water and remember what unites us—*our six basic, fundamental cultural values.*

- We have to talk to each other about our differing beliefs, listen respectfully, and try to understand why we disagree.

- Ultimately, we have to recognize and acknowledge our common bonds, and work together to solve our common problems.

My husband follows an eclectic group of contacts on social media, with political views on both the right and the left. During the pandemic, he received the exact same message from one person on the far right and one on the far left:

> *Once the Coronavirus emergency is over, every American needs to do three things:*
>
> 1. *Buy American made products.*
>
> 2. *Support your local farmers market.*
>
> 3. *Support locally owned "mom and pop" businesses and eateries.*

Incidentally, both of these individuals are entrepreneurs who own their own businesses.

Acknowledge it or not, we really are all in this together!

Question: What do you think the role of government should be during a health crisis? Have you talked with someone who is on the other side?

SOURCES

American Ways: An Introduction to American Culture Fourth Edition, by Maryanne Kearny Datesman, JoAnn Crandall, and Edward N. Kearny, Pearson Education, Inc. White Plains, NY (2014)

https://www.pewresearch.org/politics/2018/04/26/the-public-the-political-system-and-american-democracy/

https://www.ourtownsfoundation.org/

Chapter 17

CONFRONTING THE LEGACY OF SLAVERY: THE ORIGINS OF OUR DISCONTENTS

Isabel Wilkerson, a Pulitzer Prize winner and best selling author, says that we are all in some kind of *"container."* "The label signals to the world what is presumed to be inside and what is to be done with it." Her container is labeled "African-American."

Wilkerson recounts an incident that happened to her in the days "before Amazon and cell phones."

> She was doing a story for *The New York Times* about New York merchants who were opening up stores in Chicago.
>
> The man she was to interview was running late and she was waiting for him in his nearly empty boutique. As he rushed in, an employee gestured to her that he was her interviewee.
>
> The man tried to brush past her, indicating that he was late for a very important interview with *The New York Times.*
>
> Wilkerson introduced herself as *The New York Times* reporter he was waiting for, but the man did not believe her. He asked for a business card, but she had just run out of them, so he wanted to see her ID. She showed him her driver's license, but he protested that she didn't have anything with *The New York Times* on it.
>
> Finally, in exasperation, the man said, "I'm going to have to ask you to leave so I can get ready for my appointment."

Wilkerson says she left the store "dazed and incensed."

> *"This was the first time I had ever been accused of impersonating myself. His caste notions of who should be doing what in society had so blinded him that he dismissed the idea that the reporter he was anxiously awaiting, excited to talk to, was standing right in front of him. It seemed not to occur to him that a New York Times national correspondent could come in a container such as mine, despite every indication that I was she."*

What is the root of racism?

Isabel Wilkerson has given a lot of thought to racism and how the legacy of enslavement affects our lives in the 21st century. Her book *Caste:*

The Origins of our Discontents is a 2020 selection of Oprah Winfrey's book club—the most important book she's ever chosen, Oprah says. Everyone should read it.

- In her book, Wilkerson rejects "the R word" *racism* because its meaning has shifted from its sociological definition as "the combination of racial bias and systemic power" to a feeling, "a character flaw, conflated with prejudice, connected to whether one is a good person or not."

- After extensive research, Wilkerson concludes that *caste* is a better word to describe what others might call *racism*. She compares caste in the United States to that of India and the Nazis' treatment of the Jews—people are born into a "container" that forever defines them.

- She says that Americans created a caste system back in the 1600s to subjugate and control enslaved African-Americans—with white slave owners as the dominant caste and black slaves the subordinate caste.

- Wilkerson describes in agonizing detail the violence that made the lives of slaves a living hell.

- They were de-humanized, often treated worse than animals, beaten, separated from family members, and the victims of horrific medical experiments done without anesthesia; they had no individual rights whatsoever.

- And it was all legal.

What is the legacy of slavery?

After 1865, enslavement was no longer legal. However, Wilkerson believes that Jim Crow laws maintained a "caste system" of dominant whites and subordinate blacks.

- Violence continued to be used to control blacks and "keep them in their place" as the lowest members of the caste system. The KKK emerged in 1865 and soon began terrorizing African-Americans and their families.

- Lacking basic education, voting rights, and ownership of property, former slaves were prevented from lifting themselves out of poverty.

- Laws were passed that literally forbade them from learning trades and limited the types of jobs they were allowed to hold. Most were poor sharecroppers or domestic servants.

- In 1890, "85% of black men and 96% of black women were

employed in just two occupational categories, agriculture and domestic or personal service," according to the census.

- In the 1920s and '30s during the Great Migration, southern blacks began moving north to seek new factory jobs.

- However, Wilkerson observes, they "found that they could escape the South but not their caste." In the North they were relegated to the lowest level, dirtiest, lowest paying jobs, deemed appropriate to their low caste status.

- In the 20th century, violence continued across the United States, particularly in the South. Lynchings became so commonplace that they were often done in public, with the white dominant caste sometimes bringing their families to watch the spectacle.

In the 21st century, Wilkerson says this caste system is still at work, in spite of the momentous progress made during the Civil Rights Movement of the 1960s.

- This explains the subtle attitudes of the dominant white caste, making assumptions about the status and worth of blacks they do not know.

- It explains why a black Senator is stopped for questioning by the US Capitol police, even when he is wearing his Senate pin, and why Wilkerson's interviewee could not believe she was a *Times* reporter.

Why is this the time to confront the legacy of slavery?

1. The 2020s may mark a watershed moment, similar to the racial reckonings and unrest of the 1960s.

Those of us who lived through that time see many similarities.

- One important difference, however, is that so far a charismatic and determined leader like Martin Luther King, Jr., backed by the strength and human resources of the black church, has not yet emerged.

- Instead, there has been a groundswell of anger and frustration over the police treatment of African-Americans, accelerated by the killing of George Floyd.

- There was no doubt that a policeman had pressed his knee down on Floyd's neck until the black man stopped breathing—we witnessed this ghastly act over and over on TV.

- Americans were appalled and indignant.

- They had a visceral reaction and they poured into the streets to protest this grave injustice, a crowd of Americans of all ages, races, and ethnicities holding up Black Lives Matter signs.

2. The question of racial equality is on our minds. Are we a racist society? And if so, what can we do about it?

Columnist David Brooks believes we are engulfed in *a moral convulsion*, a phenomenon that seems to occur every 60 years, starting with the American Revolution. The last one was the 1960s and we are right on target for another one.

- There is a renewed movement for racial equality and justice, led by many young Americans.

- The Coronavirus Pandemic revealed startling differences between blacks and whites:

   ○ Blacks were more likely to contract the disease and more likely to die.
   ○ They had less access to healthcare, and their overall health was worse.
   ○ Many held menial jobs that were essential but put them more at risk.

Our cultural values of freedom, equality of opportunity, and the pursuit of the American Dream are at the heart of who we are. These are basic rights that all Americans should have, and it is disturbing to hear from African-Americans that many feel they still don't have them.

The practice of enslavement denied African-Americans every single one of the country's benefits: freedom, equality of opportunity, and the pursuit of the American Dream—the chance to create a better life for their children.

Slavery also denied blacks opportunities to earn these rights— through self-reliance, competition, and hard work. Their subjugation prohibited them from being independent, and their hard work benefited the slave owner, not their own families.

Before we can deal with the inequities of the present, we have to come to terms with our history. We must confront the legacy of enslavement.

Question: What do you know about slavery and what happened after the Civil War?

SOURCES

Caste: The Origins of our Discontents, by Isabelle Wilkerson, Random House, NY (2020)

https://www.nytimes.com/2020/07/31/books/review-caste-isabel-wilkerson-origins-of-our-discontents.html

https://www.npr.org/2020/08/10/900274938/caste-argues-its-most-violent-manifestation-is-in-treatment-of-black-americans

https://www.goodreads.com/book/show/51152447-caste

https://www.theguardian.com/books/2020/aug/31/caste-the-lies-that-divide-us-by-isabel-wilkerson-review

https://www.history.com/topics/early-20th-century-us/jim-crow-laws

https://www.history.com/topics/american-civil-war/reconstruction

https://www.history.com/news/lynching-museum-alabama-national-memorial-for-peace-and-justice

https://www.history.com/news/red-summer-1919-riots-chicago-dc-great-migration

David Brooks
https://www.theatlantic.com/ideas/archive/2020/10/collapsing-levels-trust-are-devastating-america/616581/

Chapter 18

CONFRONTING THE LEGACY OF SLAVERY: REPAIRING THE HOUSE DIVIDED

My father's mother was born in 1881 and grew up in an old stone farmhouse—half of it had been built in the mid-1700s and the other half dated back to the mid-1800s.

When my father took over responsibility for the house, it had been empty for a while and needed a lot of work. He discovered a major problem in the basement of the oldest part. One of the stone foundation walls was bowed out a foot or more, in spite of someone's previous attempt to buttress it with more stone.

> I remember being a teenager and standing in the basement with my father and a stonemason he had called in.
>
> The stonemason observed, "If you don't shore up this wall, it's going to collapse. It needs a retaining wall three or four feet thick built up against the side of it."
>
> "You know," he continued, "this house was built with slave labor. I can tell by the way it was done. They gathered stone from the fields and then put up the walls the best they could. It's not the work of stonemasons."

This is a historic house, built in the time of the American Revolution (before 1776) and the Civil War (1861-1865). Located in northern Virginia, it is not far from Harpers Ferry and the Antietam battlefield.

> During the Civil War, both Yankee and Rebel troops moved back and forth across the fields, and the family living in the house fed them both.
>
> When they saw soldiers coming, the family hung out the appropriate flag to welcome them—either the Union Stars and Stripes for the Northerners or the Confederate flag for the Southerners.

While my grandmother's family were southern sympathizers, my grandfather's people, living 20 miles away, fought for the North.

> My grandfather's father was actually captured and imprisoned by Confederate soldiers, while some members of my grandmother's family had fought for the Confederacy.

This became a serious issue when my grandparents fell in love.

Her parents had grave misgivings about my grandmother's marrying into a family of northern sympathizers, but they eventually agreed. My grandparents were married in 1903, after promising never to move more than a few miles from her family.

The Civil War had been part of their personal experience, but today—more than 160 years later—the ramifications of that conflict over slavery still reverberate.

What do we do with an old house?

Isabel Wilkerson says America is like an old house; there's always something that needs our attention:

- *"It should always be open for re-inspection, for additional inquiry, for checking things out, if we want it to be healthy and to stand for a long time."*

- If we ignore the problems in our old house they will fester until we have the courage to face them. We may say that personally we had nothing to do with the sins of the past; we were not here when this house was built.

- *"Our immediate ancestors may have had nothing to do with it, but here we are, the current occupants of a property with stress cracks and bowed walls and fissures built into the foundation. We are the heirs to whatever is right or wrong with it....and any further deterioration is in fact on our hands."*

The very foundation of my grandmother's house had been built by slaves, and without our repairing it, the house would have literally collapsed. Of course we did the repairs.

2020 might be remembered as an inflection moment, the time when events again forced us to confront the true dark legacy of enslavement. But how to do that?

- Is our country basically "racist" and so deeply brutal to minorities that we should rip up our founding documents and start over?

- Should that historic home be bulldozed down and a completely new modern one be built?

- Or do we need to look at the history of our American "old house" and determine what repairs we need to make? Do we have the courage to face the problems lurking there?

It's time for some tough conversations.

How do we approach the topic of enslavement?

Slavery is not a usual subject for discussion, Isabel Wilkerson says.

> *Americans are loathe to talk about enslavement in part because what little we know about it goes against our perception of our country as a just and enlightened nation, a beacon of democracy for the world. Slavery is commonly dismissed as a "sad, dark chapter" in the country's history. It is as if the greater the distance we can create between slavery and ourselves, the better to stave off the guilt or shame it induces.*

However, we have to come to terms with our history. We have to acknowledge the impact of slavery and incorporate its lessons into our historical narrative—a shared narrative that must now be inclusive, "warts and all."

Jill Lepore, a Harvard Professor of American History, has done just that in her critically acclaimed book *These Truths: A History of the United States*. The title is a reference to the Declaration of Independence:

> *We hold these truths to be self-evident, that all men are created equal, that they are endowed by their Creator with certain unalienable Rights, that among these are Life, Liberty and the pursuit of Happiness.*

Throughout her book, Lepore wrestles with this question—Have we lived up to these ideals since they were articulated for the new United States of America, or not? Have our promises been kept?

- *The American experiment rests on three ideas—"these truths," Jefferson called them—political equality, natural rights, and the sovereignty of the people. But has the nation, and democracy itself, delivered on that promise?*

- *"A nation born in contradiction… will fight, forever, over the meaning of its history," Lepore writes, "but engaging in that struggle by studying the past is part of the work of citizenship."*

The United States was indeed founded on a contradiction—the existence of slavery in a country based on the ideals of freedom and equality. Moreover, virtually all the men who wrote our founding documents—The Declaration of Independence and the Constitution—were themselves slave owners.

- Thomas Jefferson had several hundred slaves over his lifetime, although he wrote in 1781, "Nothing is more certainly written in the book of fate than that these people are to be free."

God who gave us life gave us liberty….I tremble for my country when I reflect that God is just, that his justice cannot sleep forever.

- From the early 1600s, African slaves and their white owners lived in two virtual parallel universes, "unable to separate entirely or to combine," Tocqueville observed in the 1830s. He concluded prophetically:

Although the law may abolish slavery, God alone can obliterate the traces of its existence.

Abraham Lincoln thought of our nation as "a house divided," quoting the Bible, "A house divided against itself cannot stand." The battle over legal enslavement broke the United States apart during the Civil War, and divisions still undermine our union.

How do we repair our house divided?

1. First of all, we have to remember who we are.

    - We have been a house divided from the very start.

    - Our Founding Fathers created a nation of two parallel universes, one white and one black. In the black universe, our principles of freedom, equality of opportunity, and the pursuit of the American Dream did not exist.

2. We have to remember how far we have come.

    - Slavery was abolished in 1865.

    - The Civil Rights laws of the 1960s ended legal segregation and other forms of discrimination, and protected voting rights.

3. We have to recognize how far we still have to go.

    - To some extent, those black and white parallel universes still exist—separate and unequal in certain ways.

    - A number of African-Americans still do not believe they have the freedom, equality of opportunity, or the broad access to pursuing their American Dreams that white Americans do.

    - Instances of discrimination still exist, and voter suppression may be a continuing threat.

    - Consciously or unconsciously, we may still make everyday judgments about each other based on the color of our skin.

4. We have to work together to merge those separate black/white parallel universes into one.

   • The inequities in our society—income, wealth, health, housing, schools, employment, education, poverty, social status—must be addressed.

   • This is going to require personal involvement: we have to "be the change."

   • We need to understand at an *emotional* level the impact of slavery, and how its legacy affects Americans today.

   • We may have to have the tough conversations about race and "white privilege" mentioned by Isabel Wilkerson.

5. We have to get to know each other as individuals, not as "the other."

   • We have to become friends.

   • We have to socialize together and entertain each other in our homes. We have to play together.

   • We have to build understanding and then *trust*. We have to tell each other our personal stories and share our human journeys.

In sum, we should find a way to honor Martin Luther King, Jr.'s poignant wish:

> *I have a dream that my four little children will one day live in a nation where they will not be judged by the color of their skin but by the content of their character.*

Question: What can we do as individuals to break down racial barriers and promote equality? How do we establish new friendships?

SOURCES

Caste: The Origins of our Discontents, by Isabelle Wilkerson, Random House, NY (2020)

https://www.usatoday.com/story/entertainment/books/2020/10/02/oprah-winfrey-talks-caste-author-isabel-wilkerson-racism/5894106002/

https://people.com/tv/oprahs-book-club-caste-old-house-analogy-race-in-america/

These Truths: A History of the United States, by Jill Lepore, W. W. Norton & Company, NY (2018)

https://theconversation.com/lincolns-house-divided-speech-teaches-important-lessons-about-todays-political-polarization-97841

https://www.archives.gov/founding-docs/declaration-transcript

https://flaglerlive.com/16748/i-have-a-dream-speech-mlk/

https://teachingamericanhistory.org/library/document/notes-on-the-state-of-virginia-query-xviii-manners/

https://www.pbs.org/newshour/show/an-essay-on-the-importance-of-interracial-friendships

Chapter 19

PAST, PRESENT, AND FUTURE: PATRIOTISM IS NOT A DIRTY WORD.

On a warm night in August of 1892, Francis Bellamy sat in his Boston office and contemplated his task. He was to write the words that children would recite when the flag was raised at an important ceremony—a sort of "pledge of allegiance to the flag." He was told, "It must be so fundamental, and so stirring, that it will live if possible long after this one occasion."

Bellamy said that he reflected on American history and wondered how words could be found to express our important ideals—past, present, and future.

Here is what he wrote—the original twenty-three words of the Pledge of Allegiance:

> *I pledge allegiance to my Flag and to the Republic for which it stands—one nation indivisible—with Liberty and Justice for all.*

Why did Bellamy choose these words?

Here is his explanation:

> *Of course, start it with the main idea of the moment as the children stood at salute before the flag: "I pledge allegiance to my flag," (allegiance was the great word of the Civil War period).*

> *But why allegiance to the flag? Because the flag stands for the Republic.*

> *And what does that vast thing, the Republic, mean?*

> *It is the concise political word for the Nation, the One Nation which the Civil War was fought to prove.*

> *To make that One Nation idea clearer, we must specify that it is indivisible, as Webster and Lincoln used to repeat in their great speeches.*

> *And its future?… "Liberty, equality, fraternity."*

> *No; that would be too fanciful, too many thousands of years off in realization.*

But we as a nation do stand square on the doctrine of liberty and justice for all.

That's all any one nation can handle.

So those words seemed the only roundup of past, present, and future.

And so, on October 21, 1892, on the occasion of the 400th anniversary of Columbus's voyage to the American hemisphere, tens of thousands of school children all over the United States recited the Pledge of Allegiance to the flag for the first time.

Why did the Pledge of Allegiance catch on and continue to be recited?

The historical context of the late 1800s is the key.

- By 1890, the United States was experiencing a tidal wave of immigration; for example, the public schools in New York City had more immigrant children enrolled than children born in the United States.

- How would these students from so many different countries become "Americans"?

- James Upham, a colleague of Francis Bellamy's, believed that that these students needed something tangible to symbolize the United States and inspire love of country in all the children, native as well as immigrant.

- They needed an American flag at their school, Upham believed.

- Bellamy and Upham led a "Raise the Schoolhouse Flag" campaign sponsored by the *Youth's Companion*, a popular family magazine.

- Remarkably, in one year they placed over 30,000 flags in American schools from Maine to California, wrote the Pledge of Allegiance, created a salute to the flag, and established a series of patriotic ceremonies, along with flag etiquette.

- Reciting the Pledge of Allegiance became a daily ritual for American students at the start of every school day.

- Teachers from around the nation reported that immigrant children identified with the flag and demonstrated allegiance to the United States.

When the Pledge of Allegiance was written in 1892, the United States was facing huge numbers of immigrants who brought not only different languages, but also different religions, and very different cultures. There was a need to bring people together as "Americans." The American flag and the Pledge of Allegiance were important patriotic symbols that did just that.

What about today?

Except for the addition of "under God" in the 1950s, the Pledge of Allegiance has remained unchanged for over 125 years. However, it has become controversial.

- Some American schools still require it, while others reject it.
- Some believe saluting the flag and reciting the Pledge is appropriate for civic or government meetings, while others strongly disagree.
- Some would argue that the Pledge violates the separation of church and state because of the "under God" phrase, while others proudly defend and embrace the words "under God."
- Some see it as uniting us as one people, while others protest that the phrase "with liberty and justice for all" does not in fact apply to all Americans, and it is a reminder that we have not lived up to these ideals.

Indeed, patriotism itself has become controversial.

Today, some of those on the far right are literally draping themselves in the flag, lauding the United States as the greatest country in the world—extolling historical virtues, while ignoring historical flaws.

Some of those on the far left are decrying the mistakes of the past and the inadequacies of the present, while doubting the possibilities of future change without destruction. They chant that America was never great, and they are so focused on the flaws that they have lost sight of the great American experiment and the cultural values that should inspire our love of country.

Both extremes are missing the point.

Why do we need patriotism today and tomorrow?

Mark Twain said "...modern patriotism, the true patriotism, the only rational patriotism, is loyalty to the Nation all the time, loyalty to the Government when it deserves it."

The traditional definition of patriotism is love of country and dedication to our founding ideals. It means embracing freedom, equality of opportunity, and the pursuit of the American Dream, and making a commitment to extending these rights to *all* Americans, regardless of race, creed, religion, sex, ethnicity, or national origin.

Frederick Douglass, a former slave and articulate abolitionist, wondered if the American people had patriotism enough to live up to the ideals expressed in the Constitution and the Declaration of Independence: "Are the great principles of political freedom, and of natural justice, embodied in that Declaration of Independence, extended to us?"

In the summer of 2020, in the midst of demonstrations for racial equality, there were references to a famous speech Douglas made in 1852, commemorating Independence Day:

> *"This Fourth of July is yours, not mine. You may rejoice, I must mourn. What, to the American slave, is your 4th of July? I answer: a day that reveals to him, more than all other days in the year, the gross injustice and cruelty to which he is the constant victim."*

Rodney E. Slater, one of the officials at the National Archives (where the original Declaration of Independence and the Constitution are kept), asserts that Frederick Douglass found hope in the promise of our founding documents, and so can we:

> *It is within the example of the Declaration of Independence itself that we are encouraged to stand up against oppression, challenge the status quo and continue to strive for a more perfect union. Douglass found hope in the very core of at least some of the founders' intent — to create a government of the people, by the people, and for the people — with liberty and justice for all.*

> *Frederick Douglass realized that a more perfect union begins with a promise, often stated in our most treasured documents. But it does not end there. We must make it real. We the people, sometimes with quiet determination, sometimes with righteous indignation, must move our nation to higher ground.*

In his 1963 "I Have a Dream" speech a hundred years later, Martin Luther King, Jr. again referenced the promises made by our Founding Fathers. Today, six decades later, the work to fulfill these promises continues with renewed energy, and King's words are still a call to action:

> *When the architects of our republic wrote the magnificent words of the Constitution and the Declaration of Independence, they were signing a promissory note to which every American was to fall heir. This note was a promise that all men, yes, black men as well as white men, would be guaranteed the "unalienable Rights" of "Life, Liberty and the pursuit of Happiness...."*

> *Now is the time to make real the promises of democracy....*

> *Now is the time to make justice a reality for all of God's children....*
>
> *And so even though we face the difficulties of today and tomorrow, I still have a dream. It is a dream deeply rooted in the American dream.*
>
> *I have a dream that one day this nation will rise up and live out the true meaning of its creed: "We hold these truths to be self-evident, that all men are created equal."*

On the occasion of the 50th anniversary of the Civil Rights march in Selma, Alabama, Barack Obama said,

> *"What greater form of patriotism is there than the belief that America is not yet finished, that we are strong enough to be self-critical, that each successive generation can look upon our imperfections and decide that it is in our power to remake this nation to more closely align with our highest ideals?"*

We need this form of patriotism. We need to remember who we are.

Question: What do you think about American patriotism?

SOURCES

https://vintageamericanways.com/celebrate-flag-day-today/

https://vintageamericanways.com/christopher-columbus-pledge-of-allegiance/

https://rbscp.lib.rochester.edu/3418

https://vintageamericanways.com/the-pledge-of-allegiance/

https://www.thebalance.com/american-patriotism-facts-history-quotes-4776205

https://www.usatoday.com/story/opinion/voices/2020/07/04/july-fourth-frederick-douglass-independence-day-perfect-union-column/5361907002/

https://liberalarts.utexas.edu/coretexts/_files/resources/texts/c/1852%20Douglass%20July%204.pdf

https://www.nytimes.com/2018/08/21/opinion/nationalism-patriotism-liberals-.html

https://www.americanrhetoric.com/speeches/mlkihaveadream.htm

https://obamawhitehouse.archives.gov/the-press-office/2015/03/07/remarks-president-50th-anniversary-selma-montgomery-marches

Chapter 20

FINAL THOUGHTS: WHAT ARE OUR TAKE-AWAYS?

"The Democracy! Suite" is one of jazz-great Winton Marsalis's latest compositions, written during the pandemic. In an interview on PBS, Marsalis explained the connection between jazz and the founding principles of our nation.

> *"In the way that we play jazz, we improvise, which means we have freedom.*
>
> *We swing, which means we're forced to share that freedom. And we come from a blues esthetic and blues idiom, which means that we can look into the face of something that is tragic and not paint the fake smile on it and still be optimistic about the use of our will to come together and make things better for the future."*

One of the movements of the new suite is based on the melody of the Black Lives Matter chant, and another is dedicated to Jon Baptiste, a young musician who performed in the streets during the 2020 summer protests.

Marsalis, who also teaches in top music schools, said students asked him if they had a role or a responsibility in times of civil unrest.

Marsalis said he encourages his students to be involved.

> *"I love to see them active, because, in my class, at the beginning of every year, I always ask students, what does the United States Constitution do? What is it designed to do?*
>
> *I'm always looking for them to say it's a document that's designed to level the playing field for everyone through a sophisticated system of checks and balances.*
>
> *It's important for us, as artists, to be engaged with our way of life as jazz musicians, because that's the tradition of our music."*

The interviewer was surprised that Marsalis asks his students about the Constitution—not apparently a musical question. Marsalis replied,

> *"Well, it's a musical question, because, when they don't answer it, I always say, if we don't know what our Constitution does, what chance do we have of figuring out what jazz is?"*

What does this interview with Winton Marsalis tell us?

For Marsalis, the Constitution is profoundly important: it protects our very way of life—giving us freedom and an equal chance to improve our lives. He sees these principles working in the daily lives of his students as they learn to be jazz musicians, and he believes they should understand where these ideas come from.

This is an excellent example of the relationship between the founding principles of our nation and our daily lives. It is an expression of what makes us uniquely American—our deep seated largely unconscious *cultural values*: freedom, equality of opportunity, and the pursuit of the American Dream.

- These values grew out of the immigrant experience of the first settlers in the colonial days, and they continue to draw immigrants even now.

- The writers of the Declaration of Independence and the Constitution codified these values into law, and they have endured to this day.

- The importance of freedom was first and foremost in the writers' minds, with the conviction that there were God-given rights that should apply to all people—life, liberty, and the pursuit of happiness.

- In order to secure these rights, they wrote a Constitution that begins WE THE PEOPLE in capital letters, emphasizing that the power to govern comes from the people.

- The freedom to pursue our individual happiness created the free enterprise system and our thriving economy. Indeed, these cultural values have enabled a lifestyle that is the envy of the world, with people risking their lives to come here.

But this is only part of the story. In order to have the benefits of freedom, equality of opportunity, and the pursuit of the American Dream, we have had to earn these rights and privileges.

- In order to be truly free, we have had to be self-reliant. In order to have equality of opportunity, we have had to compete for success. And in order to have the American Dream, we have had to work hard.

- You will recall that these six cultural values can be arranged in a paradigm:

Rights/Benefits	**Responsibilities/Prices to Pay**
Individual Freedom	Self-Reliance
Equality of Opportunity	Competition
The American Dream	Hard Work

While reading this book, you have taken a deep dive into these cultural values, examining where they came from, how they developed, and how they affect our daily lives.

You have also considered the failure of our country to always live up to our cultural values—to allow *all* the American people to enjoy these benefits equally.

- There has always been a chasm between our ideals and reality, with African-Americans historically living in a parallel universe of slavery, segregation, and some continuing forms of discrimination.

- Women still strive for true equality of opportunity; many Native American Indians live in economic deprivation on reservations, and minority ethnic and immigrant populations sometimes struggle against prejudice and even violence.

- People of color are often the most vulnerable in a health crisis such as the Covid Pandemic, or after a widespread weather disaster, due to where they live and work. Their families may lack adequate food, housing, health care, education, and/or employment opportunities.

- As a nation, we continue to strive for "a more perfect union" that meets the needs of *all* Americans.

What are the take-aways from this book?

First, we need to recognize that knowledge of civics is critical; the future of our democracy depends on it.

- Sandra Day O'Connor, first female Justice of the Supreme Court, has been dedicated to fostering civics education. She observed,

  "We are fortunate in the United States to have a stable and a durable democratic government. But we can't be complacent in assuming this good fortune will continue…It is the citizens of our nation who must preserve our system of government, and we cannot forget that."

- Some years ago Justice O'Conner spoke at the Chautauqua Institution and expressed her grave concern about the poor civics education in our public schools. She challenged us all to do something about it—find out what our state requirements are and demand demonstrably strong, effective civics instruction.

Second, it is essential that *all* Americans understand and embrace the foundation of our rights and freedoms.

- Conservative columnist Peggy Noonan has observed that the United States is truly unique; while other countries grew out of tribes or geographic clusters, "America was *born*—and born of *ideas.*"

- Our national identity is revealed in the *ideas* expressed in our founding documents, but we must not take our rights and freedoms for granted.

- Our system of liberties and our democratic form of government are not "a perpetual-motion machine that can run indefinitely without the attentions of the American people." The National Assessment for Educational Progress (NAEP Civics) stresses the importance of civics education:

  As Alexis de Tocqueville pointed out, each new generation is a new people that must acquire the knowledge, learn the skills, and develop the dispositions in order to maintain and improve a constitutional democracy.

- In our public schools, the NAEP for Civics measures "the civics knowledge and skills that are critical to the responsibilities of citizenship in the constitutional democracy of the United States." (See the Appendix for a summary.)

- It is our responsibility as adults to make sure our children and grandchildren have this essential knowledge, but we as adults should meet these same standards.

- It is imperative that we ourselves commit to the "values and principles" of our founding documents.

- We must do the work of citizenship.

Third, we have to come to terms with our history, warts and all.

- In *These Truths*, Jill Lapore writes that studying history is part of the work of citizenship:

  The past is an inheritance, a gift and a burden. It can't be shirked. There's nothing for it but to get to know it.

  A nation born in revolution will forever struggle against chaos.

  A nation founded on universal rights will wrestle against the forces of particularism.

  A nation that toppled a hierarchy of birth only to erect a hierarchy of wealth will never know tranquility.

A nation of immigrants cannot close its borders.

And a nation born in contradiction, liberty in a land of slavery, sovereignty in a land of conquest, will fight, forever, over the meaning of its history.

- We have to understand with empathy and compassion the legacy of slavery and its enduring effects on African-Americans today, as well as the effects of prejudice against American Asians, Native American Indians, Latinos, and other minorities.

- We have to be accountable for our actions and our words, in person and on social media.

Fourth, we have to recognize what unites us as Americans—our rights and freedoms.

- Whether we are liberal or conservative, we acknowledge that the other half of the country holds different *political* views than we do, but we must stop demonizing them for what they believe.

- This goes both ways. Both sides say that the other is a threat to our freedom, our democracy, and our way of life, but **we all want essentially the same thing—the freedom to live our lives the way we choose.**

- Using new, unique research methods to determine *private* opinions, a study by Populace, Inc. created the *American Aspirations Index*. They asked Americans to choose their personal aspirations for our country from among 55 possible choices. What factors are essential for future generations of Americans?

The results are surprising:

Across race, gender, income, education, generation, and 2020 presidential vote, there is stunning agreement on the long-term national priorities that should characterize America moving forward.

Americans agree on eight out of the top ten priorities:

1. Preserving individual rights
2. Having quality healthcare
3. Successfully addressing climate change
4. Holding political leaders accountable
5. Preserving clean water, clean air, and open spaces
6. Treating people equally in all aspects of society, regardless of background

7. Having safe neighborhoods and communities

8. Having a criminal justice system that operates without bias

Although the vast majority of Americans believe that the nation is deeply divided, they may have no idea that those on the other side of the political divide actually *share their vision* for our country!

The study concludes:

The bottom line: Across all generations; regardless of ethnicity, urbanity, and gender; whether white collar or blue collar; and even whether a viewer of CNN, MSNBC, or Fox News; nothing matters more for the long-term future of the country than upholding individual rights—upholding equal treatment for all, but not necessarily equal outcomes.

Once again, we see our three cultural values at work: *individual freedom, equality of opportunity, and the pursuit of the American Dream.*

Finally, we can no longer wait for our national leaders to solve the political division crisis. We must do our part. The ultimate solution may have to come from the bottom up, instead of from the top down. If we, as individuals, can get past the political stereotypes and recognize our common beliefs and priorities, then we can work together to solve our common problems.

Question: What are your personal priorities for the future of the United States?

SOURCES

https://www.pbs.org/newshour/show/wynton-marsalis-meets-the-moment-with-jazz-and-a-focus-on-the-nations-founding-principles

https://oconnorinstitute.org/

https://www.heritage.org/conservatism/commentary/what-patriotism

https://nces.ed.gov/nationsreportcard/civics/

These Truths: A History of the United States, by Jill Lepore, W. W. Norton & Company, NY (2018)

https://populace.org/research

https://static1.squarespace.com/static/59153bc0e6f2e109b2a85cbc/t/603d422ccfad7f5152ab9a40/1614627374630/Populace+Aspirations+Index.pdf

Chapter 21

FINAL THOUGHTS: A CALL TO ACTION

In the last few years, physical threats against members of Congress have more than doubled.

Recently, a Republican member of the House committee investigating the January 6, 2021 invasion of the Capitol received a particularly heinous threat. His wife was sent a letter from someone vowing to execute the Representative, his wife, and their newborn baby.

An unstable man broke into the home of Nancy Pelosi (Democratic Speaker of the House) in the middle of the night and attacked her husband with a hammer—fracturing his skull and injuring his arm and hand. The attacker was calling out, "Where's Nancy? Where's Nancy?" reminiscent of the January 6th Capitol invaders who were looking for Pelosi, while others were chanting, "Hang Mike Pence."

Threats of violence come from both the far right and the far left, and they have become commonplace on social media. No one seems immune.

During an election in Georgia, a woman who had volunteered to help count the votes received so many death threats that she was afraid to leave her house. She said that the threats still continue and the experience has ruined her life.

What are the consequences of these death threats and hateful acts of violence?

Historian Jon Meacham fears that our democracy is facing an existential crisis. Democracy requires us not to see each other as rivals, but as neighbors. Without that, he warns, this Great American Experiment will not continue.

StoryCorps Founder Dave Isay agrees:

> *"We've gone from disagreeing with one another to hating one another, which we and many others have come to believe may just pose an existential threat to this country because democracy cannot survive in a swamp of mutual contempt."*

> Isay blames the media "on all sides of the political spectrum profiting from our current 'culture of contempt' for one another," referring to them as the 'Hate Industrial Complex.'"

One has only to switch among news channels from CNN to MSMBC and Fox News to see diametrically opposed coverage of the same news story, highlighting our political differences. We are constantly reminded of how divided we are.

CNN commentator Michael Smerconish calls this a "collective illusion;" it reveals a profound national misunderstanding, for which the media are to blame:

> *"We reward passion. We allow those with the loudest voices to commandeer the greatest number of microphones."*

> One of his viewers agreed, tweeting, "The media and people at the extremes divide us, while the majority sits around in the middle trying to manage life."

Few of us are far left "woke" advocates, or far right extreme or "Mega MAGAs" (Make America Great Again). Indeed, the majority of Americans are truly part of what the More in Common organization calls the "Exhausted Majority." We are sick of the hateful rhetoric and divisive insults. In fact, studies continue to show that the majority of us believe that there really is more that unites us than what divides us.

But what can one individual do to bridge the divide and change the national conversation?

We can share our stories.

Dave Isay created an offshoot of StoryCorps called "One Small Step."

> *Using what they've learned over the years—about listening being an act of love—StoryCorps began a new initiative: to help connect people across these divides.*

> *"One Small Step" involves two people on different sides of the political spectrum sitting down, not to talk about politics, but rather to talk about their lives and what they have in common. The simple idea is that it is hard to hate someone who is also having trouble with a school-aged child, or who also likes to bake on the weekends, or enjoys walking his dog at sunset.*

Research shows that the key to bridging the political divide is through "conversation, empathetic listening and storytelling." Sharing our stories allows us to find our common humanity, as we seek to understand another's different perspective.

- Several years ago I co-taught a class in civil discourse. We tried to explore ways to talk about hot topics: race, religion, gender, and politics. The group wanted specific strategies and we focused on *active listening*—trying to hear *why* another person held beliefs that were contrary to our own.

- Active listening is not easy. We must concentrate on what the other is saying and not use the time to plan our rebuttal. We must repeat back our understanding of what the other one says without judgement, resisting the urge to persuade them why they are wrong.

- Active, empathetic listening also involves sharing our own stories and having a dialogue. We have to be patient, ask the other to reflect on their experience, and listen carefully to their story. Then we can share and compare our experiences.

- New experiments show that it may actually be possible to change opinions using the conversation techniques of empathetic listening and sharing stories. Two professors had success in changing voters' minds in experimental conversations called "deep canvasing."

"I think in today's world, many communities have a call-out culture," says David Broockman, a UC Berkeley political scientist who has run these experiments with Josh Kalla, a political scientist at Yale University. "Twitter is obviously full of the notion that what we should do is condemn those who disagree with us. What we can now say experimentally, the key to the success of these conversations is doing the exact opposite of that."

Psychologist Peter Coleman, who runs Columbia University's Center for Cooperation and Conflict Resolution, agrees that sharing our stories can help defuse our political confrontations. In his recent book, *The Way Out: How to Overcome Toxic Polarization*, he writes:

"...when I find myself about to react to someone who expresses political opinions opposite to mine, I stop and ask myself: 'What is my intention here? What do I hope to see happen?' This gives me a sense of control over things that often feel uncontrollable. When such conversations begin in confrontation, they often escalate quickly and become really hard to walk back. But if they begin with an opening question, or a moving story of your own experiences, they can open you both up to learning something new."

There are literally thousands of groups working to fight polarization, Coleman says:

Many are focused on facilitating community dialogues across the red-blue divide. These groups represent the immune system of our communities actively fighting against the pathologies of hate and vilification, and working to grow and mobilize the moderate middle.

How can sharing our stories help build unity in our country?

Dave Isay believes that sharing our stories is actually a form of patriotism. He hopes that one day, "One Small Step can convince America that it is our patriotic duty to listen to those with whom we disagree."

It is certainly our patriotic duty to find the humanity in each other—to get past "us" vs "them," while still celebrating the national diversity that has always been our strength.

Coco Xu is a New York research analyst for More in Common, a research and civic nonprofit that studies the forces pulling Americans apart and fosters efforts to bring them together. She recently worked on a More in Common Survey, "Fourth of July in America."

The survey found that 9 in 10 Americans reported:

> *A story of "working hard, doing your part and passing on to the next generation a better life" describes their family's experience in America.... what we all have in common is our families' resilience and the pursuit of opportunity and freedom in the U.S.*

Xu reflected on the importance of our family stories in a *Seattle Times* article, "Can we still celebrate 'E Pluribus Unum' on the Fourth of July?"

> *I strongly believe that telling the stories of "the many" is a crucial step toward living up to the Founding Fathers' motto of "E Pluribus Unum." It's also the way in which we can recognize the humanity in each other. While it does not eliminate the elements that are polarizing our politics, it helps give us a new vocabulary to disrupt the pervasive sense of us vs. them. At a time when we feel so divided, looking at our nation through the lens of family might help us see that there is still so much we all have in common — including that sacred belief that from many comes one.*

There is another important reason for sharing our stories.

Jon Meacham says that it is imperative to tell the American story of how our democracy has been able to meet the challenges of our past and move forward. For example, those of us who went through the Civil Rights Movement or the Cold War can share what we experienced.

- The younger generation must hear our stories to have optimism about their futures. We must share how we have personally overcome obstacles and have been able to persevere.

- We must also tell the stories of our nation that preserve the possibility of progress, justice, and prosperity.

- While faith in our institutions is at a low point, we have not found anything to replace them.

- In a time when only 9% of Americans believe that we can usually depend on our government to do the right thing, the vast majority of us still believe that our form of government is the best.

- We must share our belief that our form of government can still preserve our deep cultural values of individual freedom, equality of opportunity, and the pursuit of the American Dream, and that our country is worthy of our love and our commitment to its founding ideals.

Coco Xu observes,

What makes America stand out from other countries is the freedom to live out the country's ideals in the ways we choose, but also our consistent, albeit imperfect, efforts to engage with the different stories that define our families and who we are as a people. The progress we have made over time is our source of pride, as is our willingness and commitment to look at areas where we have fallen short, too.

We may be having the difficult conversations about race, ethnic prejudice, and other forms of inequality—but we must move past cancel culture to find grace and accountability, observes John Scarborough. We need accountability, but there must also be space for forgiveness and then *grace*—the ability to form new relationships and move on together, creating a new national reality.

We are once again in a time of transition in our country as we struggle to live up to our basic cultural values articulated by our founding fathers in the Declaration of Independence and the Constitution.

We are making sausage—and it is a messy, sometimes ugly process.

The good news is that we are still striving to create a country "with liberty and justice for all," in the words of the Pledge of Allegiance. The Great American Experiment continues, and our unique American cultural values are still at work!

Question: What can you do to bridge the divide?

SOURCES

https://abc7chicago.com/adam-kinzinger-wife-george-stephanopoulos-congressman/11977786/

https://chqdaily.com/2022/07/jon-meacham-shares-message-of-hope-for-future-of-american-democracy/

https://assembly.chq.org/chautauqua-lecture-series-cls/season:3/videos/jon-meacham-2022

https://fetzer.org/blog/research-behind-storycorps-one-small-step-initiative

https://www.smerconish.com/exclusive-content/america-is-not-as-divided-as-we-are-led-to-believe

http://edition.cnn.com/TRANSCRIPTS/2103/13/smer.01.html

https://www.forbes.com/sites/susanharmeling/2022/01/10/one-small-step-is-the-only-way/?sh=26b485fc6f96

https://www.vox.com/2020/1/29/21065620/broockman-kalla-deep-canvassing

The Way Out: How to Overcome Toxic Polarization, by Peter T. Coleman, Columbia University Press, NY (2021)

https://www.thewayoutofpolarization.com/about-the-book

https://www.seattletimes.com/opinion/can-we-still-celebrate-e-pluribus-unum-on-the-fourth-of-july/

More in Common "Fourth of July in America: American Identity Research Project May-June 2022" pdf https://www.moreincommon.com/

https://bridgingdivides.princeton.edu/

https://news.gallup.com/poll/394202/record-low-extremely-proud-american.aspx

https://www.cnn.com/2022/07/05/politics/decline-trust-american-institutions-poll/index.html

https://www.msnbc.com/morning-joe/watch/moving-past-cancel-culture-to-find-grace-and-accountability-108940869514

https://www.theatlantic.com/ideas/archive/2021/03/america-has-lost-ability-forgive/618336/

https://www.bgdailynews.com/community/high-performers-handle-high-stakes-conversations/article_203dc13c-3c72-597d-8b04-597224a9d8f0.html

https://www.npr.org/2021/11/09/1053929419/feel-like-you-dont-fit-in-either-political-party-heres-why

https://www.nbcnews.com/think/opinion/injustice-shaped-america-s-birth-unity-must-shape-its-future-ncna804846

Chapter 22

A PERSONAL POSTSCRIPT: SOME PRACTICAL ADVICE

You may be thinking,

What if I just don't want to deal with "those people" on the other side?

Here are some points to consider:

1. You never know when you might need a chainsaw.

The 2021 tornadoes that hit Kentucky tore through Bowling Green at one a.m. The next morning we drove to our daughter's home, where a tornado had come within a block of her house. Her neighborhood had been filled with beautiful old tall trees, many of them now lying in streets and blocking driveways, some resting on the roofs of crushed houses or tangled in downed power lines.

The air was buzzing with the sound of chainsaws. With first light, hundreds of people with chainsaws had headed into affected Bowling Green neighborhoods. When FEMA arrived, officials reportedly stood around amazed. They had never seen anything like this before! The cleanup was well underway—the people knew what to do, and they were doing it. The chainsaw volunteers didn't need to be organized; neighbors checked on each other and offered what help they could, and then they began dragging the cut tree limbs and logs onto enormous piles along the sides of streets.

Political beliefs were irrelevant.

2. You might actually be able to judge a book by its cover, but don't judge a person by their cap.

In my daughter's neighborhood, there is a small enclave of very liberal families. A few weeks after the tornado, one of the young mothers reported a surprise encounter.

There had been countless volunteers who had helped in the neighborhood—strangers who worked to clean up the downed trees, and others who brought food and water to the volunteers. All of the residents were enormously grateful for the volunteers' help.

The house across the street from this young mother had been bisected by a falling tree and she had tried to help her neighbor retrieve belongings. Having been intensely involved in the neighborhood cleanup, she was very mindful of the help from strangers.

One day she approached a stranger's truck to thank a man for his help. As she got to the truck door, she was surprised to see he was wearing a MAGA (Make America Great Again) cap! After thanking him, the liberal young mother reflected on her experience. It had given her a different perspective, she confessed. The MAGA cap was a symbol of a political orientation she despised, but she had gratitude and respect for the man who was wearing it!

We don't really know the personal beliefs of that individual in a MAGA cap, *or* the one wearing a Black Lives Matter cap, either.

3. Things are never as simple as they look. Life is complicated. People are complicated.

In Peter Coleman's book *The Way Out: How to Overcome Toxic Polarization*, he cautions us to avoid the natural human tendency to simplify. He urges us to embrace human complexity and avoid reducing "those people" (whichever side they may be on) to stereotypes.

A friend of mine, familiar with my efforts to write this book, found this anonymous post on FaceBook and passed it along. It really sums up how we all hold complicated and even contradictory beliefs:

> *For all of you who aren't sure,*
>
> *It is possible to be gay and Christian.*
>
> *It's also possible to believe in God and science.*
>
> *It is possible to be pro-choice and anti-abortion.*
>
> *It is equally possible to be a feminist and love and respect men.*
>
> *It's possible to have privilege and be discriminated against, to be poor and have a rich life, to not have a job and still have money.*
>
> *It is possible to believe in sensible gun control legislation and still believe in one's right to defend one's self, family, and property.*
>
> *It's possible to be anti-war and pro-military.*
>
> *It is possible to love thy neighbor and despise his actions.*
>
> *It is possible to advocate Black Lives Matter and still be pro-police.*
>
> *It is possible to not have an education and be brilliant.*
>
> *It is possible to be a Muslim and also suffer at the hands of terrorists.*

> *It is possible to be a non-American fighting for the American Dream.*
>
> *It is possible to be different and the same.*
>
> *We are all walking contradictions of what "normal" looks like.*
>
> *Let humanity and love win.*
>
> —Posted on Facebook, author unknown.

4. It's important to hear what the "other side" is saying about the latest news.

I have a well-educated liberal friend who has given up on the news. He lives in Washington, D.C., and used to read *The Washington Post* and *The New York Times*, often sharing clippings with his friends. He was very tuned into politics, the arts, and all the happenings in D.C.. Now he no longer reads a paper, nor does he watch any news shows on TV. He never listens to the news on the radio, nor does he read about it online. And he is proud of it. He finds the news upsetting and says he is happier not knowing what is going on.

Now, granted this is an extreme case, but most Americans limit their news intake to sources that share their political views, be it cable news, print, or online stories. Young people often prefer social media sources.

If you really want to know what's going on in America, you have to get your information from a variety of sources, conservative as well as liberal. For example, if you watch cable news, you have to at least take in CNN and Fox News to get the whole story.

This is not easy, but it has to be done. Steel yourself. If you are a conservative, you may find yourself screaming with rage at the CNN news. If you are a liberal, you may find it hard even to be in the room when Fox News is on, and you may froth at the mouth.

Hopefully, over time you will become de-sensitized, and maybe you will actually become curious about what the other side is saying.

5. Fraternizing with the enemy has its benefits.

Several years ago I joined a new community group that had political views that were different from mine. They had announced the formation of this group in the local paper, and they were looking for like-minded members. I was curious and decided to call the number in the notice. It sounded interesting, so I signed up to attend the first organizational meeting. The woman who was starting the group sent out an email with the names of the people who would be attending. I was delighted to see the names of several long-time friends on the list.

At the meeting, one of my friends said he had been surprised to see my name on the list because he knew I leaned toward the other side of the political spectrum. He and his wife concluded that I must be there because of a genuine desire to understand their concerns, which was true. It turned out that I was the only one of my political party there, but the group decided I wasn't a spy and they welcomed me.

I've been part of this organization for a number of years now and have participated in several of their projects. These are wonderful people and knowing them has enriched my life. It has given me an insight into how the "other side" thinks and a respect for their political opinions, even when I disagree with them.

Now, when a friend on my side of the political spectrum makes a generalization about what "these people" think, I have to share my experience. These are rational, complex individuals, not at all like the stereotypes attributed to them.

6. Sooner or later, you're probably going to have to deal with polarization.

That's the bad news.

Maybe you have irreconcilable differences with a family member, a colleague, or someone else that you cannot avoid interacting with. Or maybe you *want* to interact with them, but don't know where to start. What are you going to do?

The good news is that you are not alone. There are literally thousands of resources that can help you navigate through the polarization minefield—many of them are online. Try searching for "conversation across differences," for example, or "finding common ground," or "civil discourse," and see what comes up.

One of my favorite resources began several years ago as a group called "Make America Dinner Again!" The idea was to gather people who did not know each other well, have them break bread together, get acquainted, and then share conversation about topics they might not agree on.

Over time, this idea has developed into a program called *Living Room Conversations* with a wonderful interactive website. They now have over 150 conversation guides on current hot topics such as Mental Health, Abortion, Cancel Culture: Free Speech and Accountability, and Guns and Responsibility. Their website says that "belonging begins with conversation."

> *We connect people across divides—politics, age, gender, race, nationality, and more—through guided conversations proven to build understanding and transform communities.*

You can join a conversation online, organize and lead one yourself, or just read their conversation guides for ideas. There are a number of them that deal with the issue of polarization. Here's the introduction to one called "Understanding America: Political Stereotypes."

> *It can be tempting to dismiss the concerns and opinions of the people around us or to make assumptions about their motives, especially within the current political landscape. Many people have stopped talking about topics that might create discomfort due to disagreement, or even let go of connections with people they disagree with. All this can contribute to increased polarization, the reliance on information in echo chambers, and gridlock in legislative decision making. This conversation is designed to explore the assumptions and stereotypes we hold on to as well as those others might have about us. How are you navigating, being influenced by, or being impacted by current political stereotypes?*

7. Our choices determine our history.

Jon Meacham says that there never was a "once upon a time" in American history, and there will never be a "happily ever after." That's because *history is us* and the choices we make. It is the hourly, daily, weekly struggle to decide what rights to enjoy and what responsibilities we owe.

We have inherited a country that has always been flawed, but it has served us well. Now it is up to us— WE THE PEOPLE—to protect, preserve, and guarantee to all our sacred cultural values of individual freedom, equality of opportunity, and the pursuit of the American Dream.

It is up to us now. Our choices will determine the country we pass on to our children and grandchildren.

It's an awesome responsibility.

Question: What are you going to do about it?

SOURCES

The Way Out: How to Overcome Toxic Polarization, by Peter T. Coleman, Columbia University Press, NY (2021)

https://livingroomconversations.org/

https://livingroomconversations.org/topics/understanding-america-political-stereotypes/

https://assembly.chq.org/chautauqua-lecture-series-cls/season:3/videos/jon-meacham-2022

ACKNOWLEDGEMENTS

This sausage would never have been made without the aid and support of my dear friends and family.

First and foremost, I have to thank my wonderful husband George Datesman, who spent countless hours helping me do research, starting with the second, third, and fourth editions of *American Ways: An Introduction to American Culture*, which provided the foundation for *Making Sausage: Our American Values at Work*. George has read numerous books and articles for me, and he can find anything on the Internet! Most valuable of all, he has been my emotional and intellectual partner through every step of creating this book—from nagging me for over 30 years to start it, to listening to me think out loud, sharing in critical discussions, and proofreading multiple versions.

I want to also acknowledge my late husband Edward N. Kearny, who was primarily responsible for the paradigm of the six American cultural values first presented in *American Ways,* and our co-author JoAnn Crandall, who is a superstar in the field of TESOL (Teaching English to Speakers of Other Languages), a good friend, and a creative collaborator.

And now for the friends who helped make the sausage. Two of them, Ginny Lezhnev and Linda Perlis, read the first draft several years ago and were unimpressed. Actually, that version was really boring. Thank heaven for honest friends—I tore it up and started over. This approach they loved, and so I persevered. They have since read all the drafts and offered numerous helpful comments, along with other friends: Carole Clark, Edith Heins, Donna Reed, Amelia Cangemi, Maggie Brockman, Sandy Burt, Bart and Carol White, Bill Buckman, Betty Lamb, Marilyn Neuman, Maria-Nilda Cann, and Kelley Coppinger, who also designed and illustrated the cover! My deepest gratitude goes to Diane Simpson, who exercised her English-teacher skills to go over the manuscript with a fine-tooth comb, analyzing for clarity, cohesion, support, and flow. What a gift!

Amelia Cangemi and Edith Heins have been especially enthusiastic about this book, and Carole Clark has been loyally encouraging me every step of the way, hour after hour. Lynn Clark has offered a lot of guidance about his experience publishing with Amazon, and he recommended Debbi Stocco, who did an excellent job formatting this book. It was important to have a lot of white space on the pages, which complicated the process. Debbi spent many hours patiently adjusting all the bullets and quotes till they were just right. If you ever do a book for Amazon, contact Debbi Stocco! She's a phenomenal book designer and a pleasure to work with!

I am so grateful to Kelley Coppinger, Bart White, and Carol White for the many hours discussing the content of the book and what the cover should look like, and to Kelley for the stunning cover she ultimately created.

Finally, I must thank my daughter Lisa Kearny and my granddaughter Olive Lerner for their patience while I toiled on this project. Lisa gave me valuable feedback on the manuscript drafts and the space to complete *Making Sausage*. It wasn't easy, and it took several years, but I have felt called to write this book. I hope that in some small way it will contribute to civility and the strengthening of our common American bonds, as our country is passed on to my granddaughter.

APPENDIX

1. THE 100 QUESTIONS FOR THE CITIZENSHIP TEST

The 100 civics (history and government) questions and answers for the 2008 version of the civics portion of the naturalization test are listed below. The civics test is an oral test and the USCIS officer will ask the applicant up to 10 of the 100 civics questions. An applicant must answer 6 out of 10 questions correctly to pass the civics portion of the naturalization test.

On the naturalization test, some answers may change because of elections or appointments. As you study for the test, make sure that you know the most current answers to these questions. Answer these questions with the name of the official who is serving at the time of your eligibility interview with USCIS.

Although USCIS is aware that there may be additional correct answers to the 100 civics questions, applicants are encouraged to respond to the civics questions using the answers provided below.

* If you are 65 years old or older and have been a lawful permanent resident of the United States for 20 or more years, you may study just the questions that have been marked with an asterisk.

- Listen to the MP3 audio of all 100 civics questions and answers (MP3, 42.09 MB)

AMERICAN GOVERNMENT

A: Principles of American Democracy

1. What is the supreme law of the land?
Question 1 Audio (MP3, 156.91 KB)

- the Constitution

2. What does the Constitution do?
Question 2 Audio (MP3, 244.46 KB)

- sets up the government
- defines the government
- protects basic rights of Americans

3. **The idea of self-government is in the first three words of the Constitution. What are these words?**
   Question 3 Audio (MP3, 236.72 KB)

   - We the People

4. **What is an amendment?**
   Question 4 Audio (MP3, 235.91 KB)

   - a change (to the Constitution)
   - an addition (to the Constitution)

5. **What do we call the first ten amendments to the Constitution?**
   Question 5 Audio (MP3, 181.75 KB)

   - the Bill of Rights

6. **What is one right or freedom from the First Amendment?***
   Question 6 Audio (MP3, 313.28 KB)

   - speech
   - religion
   - assembly
   - press
   - petition the government

7. **How many amendments does the Constitution have?**
   Question 7 Audio (MP3, 147.13 KB)

   - twenty-seven (27)

8. **What did the Declaration of Independence do?**
   Question 8 Audio (MP3, 362.56 KB)

   - announced our independence (from Great Britain)
   - declared our independence (from Great Britain)
   - said that the United States is free (from Great Britain)

9. **What are two rights in the Declaration of Independence?**
   Question 9 Audio (MP3, 231.02 KB)

   - life
   - liberty
   - pursuit of happiness

10. **What is freedom of religion?**
    Question 10 Audio (MP3, 174.83 KB)

    - You can practice any religion, or not practice a religion.

11. **What is the economic system in the United States?***
    Question 11 Audio (MP3, 214.33 KB)

    - capitalist economy
    - market economy

12. **What is the "rule of law"?**
    Question 12 Audio (MP3, 329.98 KB)

    - Everyone must follow the law.
    - Leaders must obey the law.
    - Government must obey the law.
    - No one is above the law.

B: System of Government

13. **Name one branch or part of the government.***
    Question 13 Audio (MP3, 357.26 KB)

    - Congress
    - legislative
    - President
    - executive
    - the courts
    - judicial

14. **What stops one branch of government from becoming too powerful?**
    Question 14 Audio (MP3, 238.35 KB)

    - checks and balances
    - separation of powers

15. **Who is in charge of the executive branch?**
    Question 15 Audio (MP3, 157.31 KB)

    - the President

16. **Who makes federal laws?**
    Question 16 Audio (MP3, 283.15 KB)

    - Congress
    - Senate and House (of Representatives)
    - (U.S. or national) legislature

17. What are the two parts of the U.S. Congress?*
Question 17 Audio (MP3, 187.86 KB)

- the Senate and House (of Representatives)

18. How many U.S. Senators are there?
Question 18 Audio (MP3, 150.39 KB)

- one hundred (100)

19. We elect a U.S. Senator for how many years?
Question 19 Audio (MP3, 161.79 KB)

- six (6)

20. Who is one of your state's U.S. Senators now?*
Question 20 Audio (MP3, 360.11 KB)

- Answers will vary. [District of Columbia residents and residents of U.S. territories should answer that D.C. (or the territory where the applicant lives) has no U.S. Senators.]

21. The House of Representatives has how many voting members?
Question 21 Audio (MP3, 180.53 KB)

- four hundred thirty-five (435)

22. We elect a U.S. Representative for how many years?
Question 22 Audio (MP3, 165.05 KB)

- two (2)

23. Name your U.S. Representative.
Question 23 Audio (MP3, 422.83 KB)

- Answers will vary. [Residents of territories with nonvoting Delegates or Resident Commissioners may provide the name of that Delegate or Commissioner. Also acceptable is any statement that the territory has no (voting) Representatives in Congress.]

24. Who does a U.S. Senator represent?
Question 24 Audio (MP3, 157.31 KB)

- all people of the state

25. Why do some states have more Representatives than other states?
Question 25 Audio (MP3, 324.28 KB)

- (because of) the state's population
- (because) they have more people
- (because) some states have more people

26. **We elect a President for how many years?**
Question 26 Audio (MP3, 152.02 KB)

   - four (4)

27. **In what month do we vote for President?***
Question 27 Audio (MP3, 157.31 KB)

   - November

28. **What is the name of the President of the United States now?***
Question 28 Audio (MP3, 373.61 KB)

   - Visit uscis.gov/citizenship/testupdates for the name of the President of the United States.

29. **What is the name of the Vice President of the United States now?**
Question 29 Audio (MP3, 415.19 KB)

   - Visit uscis.gov/citizenship/testupdates for the name of the Vice President of the United States.

30. **If the President can no longer serve, who becomes President?**
Question 30 Audio (MP3, 203.74 KB)

   - the Vice President

31. **If both the President and the Vice President can no longer serve, who becomes President?**
Question 31 Audio (MP3, 232.65 KB)

   - the Speaker of the House

32. **Who is the Commander in Chief of the military?**
Question 32 Audio (MP3, 157.31 KB)

   - the President

33. **Who signs bills to become laws?**
Question 33 Audio (MP3, 158.94 KB)

   - the President

34. **Who vetoes bills?**
Question 34 Audio (MP3, 141.43 KB)

   - the President

35. What does the President's Cabinet do?
Question 35 Audio (MP3, 164.24 KB)

- advises the President

36. What are two Cabinet-level positions?
Question 36 Audio (MP3, 1.02 MB)

- Secretary of Agriculture
- Secretary of Commerce
- Secretary of Defense
- Secretary of Education
- Secretary of Energy
- Secretary of Health and Human Services
- Secretary of Homeland Security
- Secretary of Housing and Urban Development
- Secretary of the Interior
- Secretary of Labor
- Secretary of State
- Secretary of Transportation
- Secretary of the Treasury
- Secretary of Veterans Affairs
- Attorney General
- Vice President

37. What does the judicial branch do?
Question 37 Audio (MP3, 349.12 KB)

- reviews laws
- explains laws
- resolves disputes (disagreements)
- decides if a law goes against the Constitution

38. What is the highest court in the United States?
Question 38 Audio (MP3, 159.35 KB)

- the Supreme Court

39. How many justices are on the Supreme Court?
Question 39 Audio (MP3, 402.35 KB)

- Visit uscis.gov/citizenship/testupdates for the number of justices on the Supreme Court.

40. Who is the Chief Justice of the United States now?
Question 40 Audio (MP3, 429.86 KB)

- Visit uscis.gov/citizenship/testupdates for the name of the Chief Justice of the United States.

41. Under our Constitution, some powers belong to the federal government. What is one power of the federal government?
Question 41 Audio (MP3, 408.57 KB)

- to print money
- to declare war
- to create an army
- to make treaties

42. Under our Constitution, some powers belong to the states. What is one power of the states?
Question 42 Audio (MP3, 485.13 KB)

- provide schooling and education
- provide protection (police)
- provide safety (fire departments)
- give a driver's license
- approve zoning and land use

43. Who is the Governor of your state now?
Question 43 Audio (MP3, 240.39 KB)

- Answers will vary. [District of Columbia residents should answer that D.C. does not have a Governor.]

44. What is the capital of your state?*
Question 44 Audio (MP3, 375.18 KB)

- Answers will vary. [District of Columbia residents should answer that D.C. is not a state and does not have a capital. Residents of U.S. territories should name the capital of the territory.]

45. What are the two major political parties in the United States?*
Question 45 Audio (MP3, 190.3 KB)

- Democratic and Republican

46. What is the political party of the President now?
Question 46 Audio (MP3, 374.84 KB)

- Visit uscis.gov/citizenship/testupdates for the political party of the President.

47. **What is the name of the Speaker of the House of Representatives now?**
Question 47 Audio (MP3, 410.91 KB)

- Visit uscis.gov/citizenship/testupdates for the name of the Speaker of the House of Representatives.

C: Rights and Responsibilities

48. **There are four amendments to the Constitution about who can vote. Describe one of them.**
Question 48 Audio (MP3, 468.03 KB)

- Citizens eighteen (18) and older (can vote).
- You don't have to pay (a poll tax) to vote.
- Any citizen can vote. (Women and men can vote.)
- A male citizen of any race (can vote).

49. **What is one responsibility that is only for United States citizens?***
Question 49 Audio (MP3, 264.82 KB)

- serve on a jury
- vote in a federal election

50. **Name one right only for United States citizens.**
Question 50 Audio (MP3, 242.42 KB)

- vote in a federal election
- run for federal office

51. **What are two rights of everyone living in the United States?**
Question 51 Audio (MP3, 426.66 KB)

- freedom of expression
- freedom of speech
- freedom of assembly
- freedom to petition the government
- freedom of religion
- the right to bear arms

52. **What do we show loyalty to when we say the Pledge of Allegiance?**
Question 52 Audio (MP3, 237.95 KB)

- the United States
- the flag

53. **What is one promise you make when you become a United States citizen?**
Question 53 Audio (MP3, 578.79 KB)

- give up loyalty to other countries
- defend the Constitution and laws of the United States
- obey the laws of the United States
- serve in the U.S. military (if needed)
- serve (do important work for) the nation (if needed)
- be loyal to the United States

54. **How old do citizens have to be to vote for President?***
Question 54 Audio (MP3, 179.3 KB)

- eighteen (18) and older

55. **What are two ways that Americans can participate in their democracy?**
Question 55 Audio (MP3, 681.01 KB)

- vote
- join a political party
- help with a campaign
- join a civic group
- join a community group
- give an elected official your opinion on an issue
- call Senators and Representatives
- publicly support or oppose an issue or policy
- run for office
- write to a newspaper

56. **When is the last day you can send in federal income tax forms?***
Question 56 Audio (MP3, 183.78 KB)

- April 15

57. **When must all men register for the Selective Service?**
Question 57 Audio (MP3, 260.34 KB)

- at age eighteen (18)
- between eighteen (18) and twenty-six (26)

AMERICAN HISTORY

A: Colonial Period and Independence

58. What is one reason colonists came to America?
Question 58 Audio (MP3, 391.47 KB)

- freedom
- political liberty
- religious freedom
- economic opportunity
- practice their religion
- escape persecution

59. Who lived in America before the Europeans arrived?
Question 59 Audio (MP3, 192.74 KB)

- American Indians
- Native Americans

60. What group of people was taken to America and sold as slaves?
Question 60 Audio (MP3, 220.03 KB)

- Africans
- people from Africa

61. Why did the colonists fight the British?
Question 61 Audio (MP3, 356.45 KB)

- because of high taxes (taxation without representation)
- because the British army stayed in their houses (boarding, quartering)
- because they didn't have self-government

62. Who wrote the Declaration of Independence?
Question 62 Audio (MP3, 149.58 KB)

- (Thomas) Jefferson

63. When was the Declaration of Independence adopted?
Question 63 Audio (MP3, 187.86 KB)

- July 4, 1776

64. There were 13 original states. Name three.
Question 64 Audio (MP3, 659.02 KB)

- New Hampshire
- Massachusetts

- Rhode Island
- Connecticut
- New York
- New Jersey
- Pennsylvania
- Delaware
- Maryland
- Virginia
- North Carolina
- South Carolina
- Georgia

65. What happened at the Constitutional Convention?
Question 65 Audio (MP3, 244.46 KB)

- The Constitution was written.
- The Founding Fathers wrote the Constitution.

66. When was the Constitution written?
Question 66 Audio (MP3, 158.13 KB)

- 1787

67. The Federalist Papers supported the passage of the U.S. Constitution. Name one of the writers.
Question 67 Audio (MP3, 358.48 KB)

- (James) Madison
- (Alexander) Hamilton
- (John) Jay
- Publius

68. What is one thing Benjamin Franklin is famous for?
Question 68 Audio (MP3, 440.34 KB)

- U.S. diplomat
- oldest member of the Constitutional Convention
- first Postmaster General of the United States
- writer of "Poor Richard's Almanac"
- started the first free libraries

69. Who is the "Father of Our Country"?
Question 69 Audio (MP3, 138.99 KB)

- (George) Washington

70. Who was the first President?*
Question 70 Audio (MP3, 141.03 KB)

- (George) Washington

B: 1800s

71. What territory did the United States buy from France in 1803?
Question 71 Audio (MP3, 252.61 KB)

- the Louisiana Territory
- Louisiana

72. Name one war fought by the United States in the 1800s.
Question 72 Audio (MP3, 360.93 KB)

- War of 1812
- Mexican-American War
- Civil War
- Spanish-American War

73. Name the U.S. war between the North and the South.
Question 73 Audio (MP3, 240.8 KB)

- the Civil War
- the War between the States

74. Name one problem that led to the Civil War.
Question 74 Audio (MP3, 273.37 KB)

- slavery
- economic reasons
- states' rights

75. What was one important thing that Abraham Lincoln did?*
Question 75 Audio (MP3, 359.71 KB)

- freed the slaves (Emancipation Proclamation)
- saved (or preserved) the Union
- led the United States during the Civil War

76. What did the Emancipation Proclamation do?
Question 76 Audio (MP3, 386.99 KB)

- freed the slaves
- freed slaves in the Confederacy
- freed slaves in the Confederate states
- freed slaves in most Southern states

77. What did Susan B. Anthony do?
Question 77 Audio (MP3, 235.09 KB)

- fought for women's rights
- fought for civil rights

C: Recent American History and Other Important Historical Information

78. Name one war fought by the United States in the 1900s.*
Question 78 Audio (MP3, 382.92 KB)

- World War I
- World War II
- Korean War
- Vietnam War
- (Persian) Gulf War

79. Who was President during World War I?
Question 79 Audio (MP3, 160.57 KB)

- (Woodrow) Wilson

80. Who was President during the Great Depression and World War II?
Question 80 Audio (MP3, 199.67 KB)

- (Franklin) Roosevelt

81. Who did the United States fight in World War II?
Question 81 Audio (MP3, 203.74 KB)

- Japan, Germany, and Italy

82. Before he was President, Eisenhower was a general. What war was he in?
Question 82 Audio (MP3, 220.84 KB)

- World War II

83. During the Cold War, what was the main concern of the United States?
Question 83 Audio (MP3, 203.33 KB)

- Communism

84. What movement tried to end racial discrimination?
Question 84 Audio (MP3, 172.79 KB)

- civil rights (movement)

85. What did Martin Luther King, Jr. do?*
Question 85 Audio (MP3, 240.8 KB)

- fought for civil rights
- worked for equality for all Americans

86. What major event happened on September 11, 2001, in the United States?
Question 86 Audio (MP3, 230.21 KB)

- Terrorists attacked the United States.

87. Name one American Indian tribe in the United States.
Question 87 Audio (MP3, 1.13 MB)

[USCIS Officers will be supplied with a list of federally recognized American Indian tribes.]

- Cherokee
- Navajo
- Sioux
- Chippewa
- Choctaw
- Pueblo
- Apache
- Iroquois
- Creek
- Blackfeet
- Seminole
- Cheyenne
- Arawak
- Shawnee
- Mohegan
- Huron
- Oneida
- Lakota
- Crow
- Teton
- Hopi
- Inuit

INTEGRATED CIVICS

A: Geography

88. Name one of the two longest rivers in the United States.
Question 88 Audio (MP3, 230.21 KB)

- Missouri (River)
- Mississippi (River)

89. What ocean is on the West Coast of the United States?
Question 89 Audio (MP3, 183.78 KB)

- Pacific (Ocean)

90. What ocean is on the East Coast of the United States?
Question 90 Audio (MP3, 182.16 KB)

- Atlantic (Ocean)

91. Name one U.S. territory.
Question 91 Audio (MP3, 348.71 KB)

- Puerto Rico
- U.S. Virgin Islands
- American Samoa
- Northern Mariana Islands
- Guam

92. Name one state that borders Canada.
Question 92 Audio (MP3, 624.4 KB)

- Maine
- New Hampshire
- Vermont
- New York
- Pennsylvania
- Ohio
- Michigan
- Minnesota
- North Dakota
- Montana
- Idaho
- Washington
- Alaska

93. Name one state that borders Mexico.
Question 93 Audio (MP3, 287.63 KB)

- California
- Arizona
- New Mexico
- Texas

94. What is the capital of the United States?*
Question 94 Audio (MP3, 169.94 KB)

- Washington, D.C.

95. Where is the Statue of Liberty?*
Question 95 Audio (MP3, 316.54 KB)

- New York (Harbor)
- Liberty Island

[Also acceptable are New Jersey, near New York City, and on the Hudson (River)]

B: Symbols

96. Why does the flag have 13 stripes?
Question 96 Audio (MP3, 281.52 KB)

- because there were 13 original colonies
- because the stripes represent the original colonies

97. Why does the flag have 50 stars?*
Question 97 Audio (MP3, 308.8 KB)

- because there is one star for each state
- because each star represents a state
- because there are 50 states

98. What is the name of the national anthem?
Question 98 Audio (MP3, 169.94 KB)

- The Star-Spangled Banner

C: Holidays

99. When do we celebrate Independence Day?*
Question 99 Audio (MP3, 220.25 KB)

- July 4

100. Name two national U.S. holidays.
Question 100 Audio (MP3, 926.94 KB)

- New Year's Day
- Martin Luther King, Jr. Day
- Presidents' Day
- Memorial Day
- Independence Day
- Labor Day
- Columbus Day
- Veterans Day
- Thanksgiving
- Christmas

https://www.uscis.gov/citizenship/find-study-materials-and-resources/study-for-the-test/100-civics-questions-and-answers-with-mp3-audio-english-version   Last Reviewed/Updated: 09/16/2021

2. THE FIRST 10 AMENDMENTS TO THE UNITED STATES CONSTITUTION: THE BILL OF RIGHTS

What are the individual rights specified in the Bill of Rights?

1. Freedom of religion, speech, and the press; the right to peaceably assemble and petition the government about grievances:

> *Congress shall make no law respecting an establishment of religion, or prohibiting the free exercise thereof; or abridging the freedom of speech, or of the press, or the right of the people peaceably to assemble, and to petition the Government for a redress of grievances.*

This First Amendment is often cited as one of our most important—it protects our freedoms from the power of the government.

It guarantees our right to practice our religion as we wish, and to criticize the government, speaking as individuals or in the press.

It also means that the government cannot stop us from having peaceful demonstrations or advocating for changing unfair laws.

2. The right to bear arms:

> *A well regulated Militia, being necessary to the security of a free State, the right of the people to keep and bear Arms, shall not be infringed.*

The interpretation of this amendment is often the subject of heated debate. Most Americans would probably agree that it gives us the right to own and use guns. But does it guarantee our right to have guns of any type, including automatic weapons?

If the original intent was to legalize guns needed for participating in a government militia, how does that affect the regulation of gun ownership today?

3. Quartering of soldiers (limitations on soldiers being housed in private homes):

> *No Soldier shall, in time of peace be quartered in any house, without the consent of the Owner, nor in time of war, but in a manner to be prescribed by law.*

The Third Amendment was important to the original colonists because the British had forced private citizens to house soldiers. It specifies that the American government can only do this is a time of war and after passing laws to regulate the practice.

4. The right to be free from unreasonable search or arrest:

> *The right of the people to be secure in their persons, houses, papers, and effects, against unreasonable searches and seizures, shall not be violated, and no Warrants shall issue, but upon probable cause, supported by Oath or affirmation, and particularly describing the place to be searched, and the persons or things to be seized.*

The Fourth Amendment prevents the government from searching individuals, their homes, papers, and personal items without a warrant indicating probable cause of some wrongdoing.

The definition of what constitutes an "unreasonable" search or seizure has been subject to some interpretation.

5. Individual rights in criminal cases:

> *No person shall be held to answer for a capital, or otherwise infamous crime, unless on a presentment or indictment of a Grand Jury, except in cases arising in the land or naval forces, or in the Militia, when in actual service in time of War or public danger; nor shall any person be subject for the same offence to be twice put in jeopardy of life or limb, nor shall be compelled in any criminal case to be a witness against himself, nor be deprived of life, liberty, or property, without due process of law; nor shall private property be taken for public use, without just compensation.*

The Fifth Amendment is certainly one of the most famous. Taking the Fifth—"I refuse to answer on the grounds that it may incriminate me"—is a line we hear often on TV.

The government cannot compel us to testify against ourselves in court or in front of bodies such as Congress and the FBI.

This Amendment also requires the government to obtain an indictment by a Grand Jury before charging an individual with a crime.

The accused is considered innocent until proven guilty, and if found innocent may not be tried again—that is, put in "double jeopardy."

And the government may not seize private property for public use without paying a fair price for it.

6. The right to a fair trial in criminal cases:

In all criminal prosecutions, the accused shall enjoy the right to a speedy and public trial, by an impartial jury of the State and district wherein the crime shall have been committed; which district shall have been previously ascertained by law, and to be informed of the nature and cause of the accusation; to be confronted with the witnesses against him; to have compulsory process for obtaining witnesses in his favor, and to have the assistance of counsel for his defense.

The Sixth Amendment spells out our rights if we are accused of a crime:

- to have a speedy, public trial by jury;
- to be tried in the vicinity of where the crime was committed;
- to be told what crime is alleged;
- to be able to confront the witnesses for the prosecution;
- to have a way to compel defense witnesses to testify;
- and to have a defense attorney.

7. Rights in civil cases:

In Suits at common law, where the value in controversy shall exceed twenty dollars, the right of trial by jury shall be preserved, and no fact tried by a jury shall be otherwise re-examined in any Court of the United States, than according to the rules of the common law.

The Seventh Amendment guarantees the right to a trial by jury in certain civil cases. However, most civil cases are now prosecuted at the state level and are settled by a judge.

8. Bails, fines, and punishments:

Excessive bail shall not be required, nor excessive fines imposed, nor cruel and unusual punishments inflicted.

The Eighth Amendment protects us against excessive bails and fines, as well as cruel and unusual punishment.

9. Rights retained by the people:

The enumeration in the Constitution of certain rights shall not be construed to deny or disparage others retained by the people.

The Ninth Amendment asserts that just because certain rights are specifically listed in the Constitution, it does not mean that other rights not enumerated don't exist.

10. States' rights

The powers not delegated to the United States by the Constitution, nor prohibited by it to the States, are reserved to the States respectively, or to the people.

Finally, the Tenth Amendment says that any power not specifically given to the Federal government by the Constitution shall be reserved to the states (unless prohibited by the Constitution) or to the people of the United States.

3. WHAT DOES THE NAEP CIVICS ASSESSMENT MEASURE?

The NAEP (National Assessment for Educational Progress) Civics Assessment measures the civics knowledge, skills, and dispositions that are critical to the responsibilities of citizenship in America's constitutional democracy. The assessment is administered to students at grades 4, 8, and 12. In 2014 and 2018, the assessment was administered only at grade 8.

The NAEP Civics Framework, the blueprint for the assessment, was developed by the National Assessment Governing Board and recommends that the assessment should be organized around three main components: knowledge, intellectual and participatory skills, and civic dispositions. A brief description of each component follows.

Civic Knowledge

The civic knowledge component draws heavily on the National Standards for Civics and Government developed by the Center for Civic Education and covers the broad range of content that forms the basis of civic understanding. It is organized into five main categories, expressed as questions.

- What are civic life, politics, and government?
- What are the foundations of the American political system?
- How does the government established by the Constitution embody the purpose, values, and principles of American democracy?
- What is the relationship of the United States to other nations and to world affairs?
- What are the roles of citizens in American democracy?

These essential content questions denote basic concepts about the theory and practice of constitutional democracy in the United States, which students need to know to become informed and responsible citizens.

Civic Skills

Intellectual and participatory civic skills involve the use of knowledge to think and act effectively and in a reasoned manner in response to the challenges of life in a constitutional democracy.

Intellectual skills enable students to learn and apply civic knowledge in the many and varied roles of citizens.

- These skills help citizens identify, describe, explain, and analyze information and arguments,
- as well as evaluate, take, and defend positions on public issues.

Participatory skills enable citizens to monitor and influence public and civic life by working with others,

- clearly articulating ideas and interests,
- building coalitions,
- seeking consensus,
- negotiating compromise,
- and managing conflict.

Civic Dispositions

The third component of this framework, civic dispositions, refers to the inclinations or "habits of the heart," as de Tocqueville called them, that pervade all aspects of citizenship. In a constitutional democracy, these dispositions pertain to the rights and responsibilities of individuals in society and to the advancement of the ideals of the polity.

They include the dispositions to

- become an independent member of society;
- respect individual worth and human dignity;
- assume the personal, political, and economic responsibilities of a citizen;
- participate in civic affairs in an informed, thoughtful, and effective manner;
- and promote the healthy functioning of American constitutional democracy.

From the *Civics Framework for the 2018 National Assessment for Educational* Progress, published by the National Assessment Governing Board, U.S. Department of Education.

www.ingramcontent.com/pod-product-compliance
Lightning Source LLC
Chambersburg PA
CBHW081255130726
47998CB00010B/2803